Meeting Jesus

Three Christmas Stories

MEETING JESUS

THREE CHRISTMAS STORIES

CLEO LAEL

Meeting Jesus: Three Christmas Stories by Cleo Lael
Copyright © 2018 by Cleo Lael
All Rights Reserved.
ISBN: 978-1-59755-481-7

Published by: ADVANTAGE BOOKS™
Longwood, Florida, USA
www.advbookstore.com

This book and parts thereof may not be reproduced in any form, stored in a retrieval system or transmitted in any form by any means (electronic, mechanical, photocopy, recording or otherwise) without prior written permission of the author, except as provided by United States of America copyright law.

Library of Congress Catalog Number: 2018959043
1.   Religion / Christian Life / Inspirational

First Printing: October 2018
18 19 20 21 22 23 24   10 9 8 7 6 5 4 3 2 1
Printed in the United States of America

Table of Contents

The Guests in the Stable 5
A Shepherd Tale 29
At the End of the Journey 65
End Notes 109

Cleo Lael

The Guests in the Stable

Judah stood and looked out the open window at the street below. People pushed, shoved, and shuffled about. Judah had never seen Bethlehem so full. The noise sounded monstrously loud, but he knew that it would be deafening if he were in the street below. All the spare rooms he considered full, but they were still making room for more.

"Judah! What are you doing just standing there? You have work to do," scolded Samuel.

Judah sighed and hurried way. Samuel was an elder in the town and an old, distant relative of his. Twelve-year-old Judah and his six-year-old sister Hadassah had been living with him ever since their family had died. The fast-moving illness had killed nearly everyone in their village. Because Samuel was a relative they had come to live with him. Judah and Hadassah were not slaves since they lived with a relative, but sometimes Judah felt like they worked more like servants, and no one cared about them. He knew Samuel had other things to worry about and really did care about them. Judah should be grateful for all he did have, but life had not been easy or very kind to him. Judah pushed that thought to the back of his mind and hurried on his way.

Judah did not have any time to think of much more than the tasks at hand for the next two days. If he had thought things were busy before; they were crazy now. The house was beyond full. There were bodies everywhere, and Judah thought the house might just burst from it all. Because Samuel was a prominent man in Bethlehem his house was where guests and visitors stayed. For this reason they often had strangers in the house but never this many. Judah saw Hadassah a few times, but she was often kept in the kitchen or busy elsewhere. Judah did what he could where he could, but all the people were driving him crazy. Late in the afternoon Judah found himself with nothing to do. There were too many people everywhere, and he could not find anything to do. When Samuel asked him why he was not working, Judah explained he did not know what to do.

"Go help Martha in the kitchen or whatever she may need help with," Samuel said. But at that moment Martha showed up out of nowhere.

"Oh, no you don't," she scolded. "I don't need him in the kitchen. There are too many bodies there, and the last thing we need is another one shoving about." And with that she was off again.

"Very well, why don't you go out and sweep off the stairs and make things look nice outside," said Samuel.

"Yes, Samuel," replied Judah, and he hurried off. It was loud and crazy outside too, but it had to be better than in the house thought Judah. Soon he was outside sweeping the steps. It seemed pointless because there was no way to get rid of all the dirt.

The noise was amazing. Everyone was shouting and yelling. He could hear two men in a heated argument. A woman was scolding her child and in return got scolded by her husband. A baby was crying not too far away which turned into a full-fledged scream. Judah's ears were nearly ringing out here, but at least on the steps he was not pressed by other bodies. If he dared enter into the street he would be.

Judah's mind drifted back to when he first learned that this would happen. That day Samuel had told everyone to prepare to have a lot of visitors. When asked how many, Samuel said as many as the house would hold. The Roman Empire had declared a census that every man had to be registered. Later Judah had asked Samuel to explain more. He explained that the nation of Judea was no longer its own country. Most Jews were not happy with this. Now the Roman Empire wanted to count the people, maybe for taxes, maybe just to know how many people there were. Every man had to register in a certain town or city depending on their ancestry. Bethlehem was the city of King David, so all from the line of David had to come to Bethlehem to register.

Now the people were here, and Bethlehem was packed. Samuel had already turned people away because the house was too full as it was. Judah looked out across the crowd. The street was a sea of people. Then he noticed a man slowly walking along with a young woman by his side. At first Judah barely noticed them, but as they got closer he saw the man look up at the house, turn to the girl, and point. Then he started guiding her toward the house. He walked up to the house, stopped and talked to the girl. She nodded and placed a hand on her swollen stomach, and for the first time Judah realized she was with child. The man then started walking up the stairs, leaving her standing below. He walked slowly, like he was very tired. When he reached Judah he asked,

"Is this still the home of Samuel son of Abijah?"

"Yes, Sir," Judah replied.

"Is there any room left?"

"No, Sir," Judah told him. He felt bad, with the lady being with child and all, but there was nothing he could do. With this many people, he was sure that every house would be full.

The man sighed and glanced over his shoulder at the girl. "May I speak with Samuel please?" he asked.

"I'll go find him," Judah replied and headed off. He hurried around the house and pushed past people to try and find Samuel. Judah finally found him and told him, "There is a man outside who wants to talk to you."

"What does he want?"

"I think he wants a room."

"Tell him we are full."

"I did, Sir."

"Well, tell him again."

"I think he may know you, Sir, and his wife is with child."

"How far along is she?"

"From what I could see, Sir, she looks like she could have it any day."

Samuel sighed and straightened up. "All right," he said and followed Judah outside. When they got outside, Judah grabbed the broom and made himself look busy, but really he was listening to the conversation. It went like this.

"Hello, Samuel," the stranger said.

"Why, hello, Joseph! I forgot that you would have to come here. How are you?"

Joseph gave Samuel a faint smile, "Tired," he said.

"And who is that with you?"

"Mary."

"So you got yourself married, eh?"

"I was hoping you had some place we could stay, but the boy tells me not."

Samuel looked down, then back up at Joseph and frowned. "If I had remembered you would be coming, I would have saved a place for you. I know you don't have any family in this area anymore. I am really sorry, Joseph," he said. Then Samuel repeated what Judah had been thinking earlier. "With this many people here, I doubt anyone has room anymore."

Joseph sighed again. "It's not so much for me, but Mary. She is expecting any day. I know other people may be willing to take us in, but I don't want to stay with strangers. Some people may even have to camp in the open, with how full it is, but I don't want to camp out in the open. There are going to be thieves and robbers with this many people around, you know. I will have to take care of things for the census during the day, so I will have to leave her alone." Joseph looked long and hard at Samuel before he spoke again. "Please, Samuel, I'm begging you. I have nothing else I can do, or anywhere else to go. Please, Samuel!"

"Let me think for a minute," Samuel replied. Both men were quiet for a moment, and Samuel paced back and forth. When he stopped and looked up, Joseph looked hopeful. "I don't think you will like this idea, but it is all I can think of," Samuel said.

"What?" asked Joseph.

"The stable area," said Samuel. "It will be full of the other people's animals, and it is not the cleanest, but it is warm and will be safe."

Joseph thought about it for a minute and then said, "I will have to talk with Mary about it."

Joseph walked back down the stairs and started to talk with Mary. Judah saw her head nod, and Joseph walked back up the stairs and said they would take it. Samuel turned to Judah and told him to go with them. He was to look after them and get anything they needed.

"If you need anything at all just tell Judah, and he can get it for you. He will be sleeping in the stable with you tonight."

Judah thought about the stable. It was the first floor of the house. When one walked in the door it sloped down and gave way to stalls. At this time Samuel had a cow for milk, and a donkey of his own, and a few sheep that could be eaten later. Now it was full of the guest's animals. They were mostly donkeys, but there was one horse and one camel. They were kept at opposite ends of the stable for fear that they may not get along. There was a small area to one side that was elevated a little for the caretaker of the animals to sleep on. Judah usually slept there.

"Judah!" Samuel yelled, and Judah snapped out of his own thoughts and back to the present again. He then set the broom against the house and hurried down the steps after Joseph. Joseph helped Mary walk down into the stable area, and Judah led them over to the area where he usually slept. As Joseph doted over Mary, Judah hurried around to get extra blankets and things they could use.

Mary looked up at Judah and glancing at Joseph, she asked, "And who is this?"

"Oh, this is a young boy Samuel told to look after us. What is your name again?" Joseph asked.

"Judah, Sir."

"Oh, you need not call me Sir, Joseph is just fine," Joseph told him. "And, this is Mary."

Mary smiled warmly at Judah. Looking at her, Judah could feel his heart begin to ache. She looked a little like his own older sister. Both girls would have been about the same age, and his sister had been betrothed too. But she had died with the rest of his family. The man she was betrothed to had died as well. Judah bowed his head, and although it hurt, he did not cry. He had not cried since his family had died. Judah took a deep breath and did his best to shake away the memories and focus on the present. "Is there anything I can get you? Maybe some food from the kitchen?" Judah asked.

"Something to eat would be nice," Mary said.

Judah nodded and hurried away. Now was not the time to think about the past, but then again he never let himself think about it. Once again he shook his head and ran out. He managed to slip into the kitchen and was gathering some food when Martha walked in.

"Just what do you think you are doing?" she scolded.

"We have guests in the stable below. Samuel has me taking care of them, and this food is for them," Judah explained.

"How many?"

"A man and a women, but the lady is with child."

"How far along is she?"

"She looks like she could burst any day."

Martha nodded, then looking back at Judah, she scolded, "Well, why are you just standing there? Go take that to them!"

Judah hurried off. Martha was always yelling and scolding everyone, even when she did not mean it. He had gotten used to it.

When he got back to the stable, Joseph was unpacking and arranging their things. Judah gave them the food, and they both began to slowly eat. Joseph offered him some of the food, but Judah told him that he would eat later. In truth Judah was not sure when he would get to eat.

"I will sleep up in that corner over there tonight with the feed and extra hay," he told them. After they finished eating, Judah helped Joseph fix things up. Mary soon lay down and fell asleep. Judah was about to leave and see if he could get something to eat when Joseph pulled him off to the side.

"For the next two days at least, I will be taking care of things with the census and such. I don't want Mary to be alone with the child so close to being born. I would like it if you could stay with her," Joseph asked.

"Yes, Sir," Judah responded.

"You don't need to keep calling me sir, and thank you so very much," Joseph said. Then, half under his breath, Judah heard him say, "This child is very special."

When Judah got back from getting something to eat, he found them both asleep, so he curled up in his own corner. He could hear the noise

The Guests in the Stable

from the people above him, but Judah was so tired he soon fell asleep too.

In the morning Judah got them some more food then Joseph hurried off. Judah had talked to Samuel about what Joseph had asked him to do, and Samuel told him to stay with Mary. He also gave Judah something to do while he was down there. As Judah worked he tried to make small talk with Mary. He liked her already. She was sweet and nice. He often asked how she was, and she always smiled and said she was fine. She always spoke of the baby as a boy.

"What will his name be?" Judah asked. Mary looked up, and her gaze seemed to drift as if she was far away.

"His name will be Jesus," she replied.

"Did Joseph give him that name?"

"No."

Judah thought it a little strange. Usually the father would name the child, but what did that matter. "Well I bet that Joseph is very proud."

Mary sighed. "If I tell you something, will you promise not to tell anyone? Those who do know don't want to talk about it, but I don't want it getting out all over Bethlehem."

"I can keep a secret," Judah promised.

Mary looked right at him. "The child is not Joseph's."

Judah did not think he could have been more surprised if Mary had just sprouted wings in front of him. He just stared at her. Mary smiled and said, "Joseph knows."

"Were you married before…?"

"No. Maybe I should explain more. It all stared with, well," she paused, "well, when the angel appeared to me."

Judah was wrong. Now he was more surprised. He just stared at Mary for a little. "An Angel!!!!"

Mary smiled again. "Yes, an angel. Nine months ago I was still just betrothed to Joseph. I was living in my father's house in Nazareth when the angel appeared to me. The angel started by greeting me and saying that the LORD was with me. I, of course, was frightened by him but also by his words. I wondered what kind of greeting this was. Why was an angel appearing to me, of all people? Was this good, or was it bad?

11

He said the Lord was with me. Then he said not to be afraid, that I had found favor with God, like God was pleased with me. Then he said (of all things) that I would have a son, and his name was to be Jesus, and it sounded like he was to be a king and reign forever. I know everything the angel said, but I did not really know what he meant. I still am not really sure."

"My first thought went to the fact that I was not married and had never been with a man, so this could not possibly happen. I told the angel this, and he said that the Holy Spirit would come upon me and the Most High would over shadow me, and because of this, the child would be called the Son of God. I did not know what all that meant, but it almost sounded like the child would be the son of God, but I don't know if that is possible. Then the angel reassured me by telling me that my relative Elizabeth was with child. Now, you see, Elizabeth is old and has been barren all her life. But the angel said she was in her sixth month. Then he said that nothing is impossible for God. I just stood there for a little, stunned. But I thought about Samson's mother being told by an angel she would have a son, and Samuel's mother Hannah was given by God, the child she asked for. I did not understand all that was said, but it would seem I was to be with child soon. I also thought that if this is God's will then who am I to stand against it, so I said that I was the LORD's slave girl, let it happen to me as he said. Then the angel was gone."

Judah just stared at Mary, not sure what to think or say.

"Maybe it would help if I told you exactly what the angel said to me, and what I said back." Judah nodded and listened closely as she told it all again, word for word what the angel said. Judah could do nothing but stare. It seemed so wild that it could just maybe be true. It would take a lot to make up a story like this, and Mary did not seem like the type to make up wild stories.

After she finished telling it all again, she continued on. "After the angel left, I half wondered if I had dreamed it all or imagined it. So I convinced my parents to let me go see Elizabeth. I traveled as quickly as I could but even in that time I knew something strange was happening inside me. Somehow I knew the angel's words were coming true. When I got to Elizabeth's house I went in, and when I saw her, I called out and greeted her, and do you know what she did?" Mary asked. Judah shook his head still trying to wrap it around what he was hearing. "She cried out in a loud voice that I was blessed among women and blessed was the fruit of my womb! I was shocked. I could see that she was indeed with child. Then she asked why the mother of her Lord would come to see her. Before I could answer she explained that when she heard my voice her own baby had jumped for joy inside her. Then she said that I was blessed again because I believe what I was told by the Lord. I did believe what I was told. There is just no way to not believe an angel, but I went to see Elizabeth just to make sure. Then I sang to God because of what He did for me. He thought of me of all people, and He gave me a way to see His truth through Elizabeth. So I sang to God this song." Then Mary began to sing a song that Judah had never heard. It sounded like a psalm from King David. It was beautiful and sweet, and Judah found himself caught up in it. He was sad when it ended and wished it would go on. He smiled at Mary, and then he said,

"That was wonderful, but what about Joseph? I can't image him being very happy when he found out."

Mary shook her head sadly and continued her story. "I stayed there for three months, then I went home. By now I was with child, and it was not very hard to tell. In a small town like Nazareth, word gets around fast. I did not tell anyone, but it still got out. My parents were furious and terrified. You know the law, and because I was betrothed to Joseph he could have had me killed for this. If he did not clam the child as his own, I could be doomed. Joseph refused to talk with me at first. He was too shocked."

"Were you scared?" Judah asked.

"Oh, very," Mary responded. "Even my own parents could have had me stoned. I told them about the angel and all he had said, and about Elizabeth. I told them everything, but they didn't really believe me. I mean, the story sounds crazy to my own ears, but it was the truth so what else could I say? I don't know what happened to Joseph during this time. He told me later it was one of the hardest times of his life. He loved me, but he did not believe my story even though there was no other explanation. I remember the morning he came to the house and asked to talk to me alone. I was so scared. I felt like I had let him down but what else could I do? The LORD had spoken, and who was I to disagree, even if it cost me everything. I mean, is that not what the prophets went through?" She asked, pausing to take a long breath.

Judah just sat there thinking. Had God really talked to this lady? And what did it all mean? He did not have time to think on it now because Mary started up her story again.

"We took a walk out through one of the fields. At first we did not talk, but then he stopped and told me that he believed me. I was so surprised that I just stared at him. He told me that an angel had come to him in a dream and told him not to be afraid to take me has his wife, that the child did come from the Holy Spirit. It would be a son, and he was to give him the name Jesus. He said that we were to name him that because this child would save his people from their sins."

Judah could not stop staring at her. "Does that mean he is to be... the... well, Messiah?" he asked in amazement.

"I think maybe," replied Mary. "Joseph talked with my parents that day, and I went to live with him as his wife. He never really claimed the child as his, but that is what everyone took it to mean. With the town being so small, gossip flies around and no one forgets anything."

"Things have been really rough for you guys, hasn't it?" Judah said.

"Yes it has, but I know we are doing what God has told us to do, so I am not too worried," replied Mary.

Judah and Mary continued to talk about what life had been like for them in the last couple months. He continued to work, and later Mary said she would like to walk up to the house for a little while. Judah helped her up to the house were they ate a little. He was in and out for the rest of the day.

Joseph came back sooner than Judah had expected, but he explained there was nothing more he could do for the day. Judah hurried up to the main part of the house to get some food for him, but it took longer than he expected, and when he made it back down, Mary was asleep.

Joseph smiled and thanked him for the food. "Mary was tired, and it is just as well she rests. The trip was hard on her."

"She did not have to come along, did she?" Judah asked.

"No, but she did not want to stay back alone, being with child and all," he said. "I can't blame her, and I did not have the heart to tell her no." Joseph smiled at him again. "She told me she told you the child's story so far."

Judah looked up and nodded nervously. "She did," he said. Joseph smiled understandingly down at him. Judah mustered his courage and asked, "How did you feel when you found out?"

"That Mary was with child?" Joseph asked. Judah nodded. "Betrayed," he said. "I did not understand. We were betrothed and I loved her. I looked forward to her being my wife and being around her every day. She was all I wanted in a wife. We had known each other for some time. I remember being surprised when I found out she wanted to go to Judea to visit a family member. When I questioned her why, she just said it was something she needed to do. When she came back, a friend ran to tell me she was back and was with child. I thought he was joking, and I hurried to see her. But when I did, I saw it was no joke. I was so shocked I just stood there and stared. Then she lifted her head and our eyes met."

Joseph stopped and ran a hand over his face. Judah could see the emotion on his face and how it all seemed to be real again for him. Joseph took a ragged breath and continued. "We just stared at each other for a bit then I turned away. She called out to me, but I did not turn back. I half ran out of town. I went on a long walk and talked to God, or should I say, yelled at God. That day and the days that followed were some of the worst in my life. I did not understand. Why had this happened? I did not want to believe it, but it was true. I heard her story and scoffed at it. I wanted to believe it but really, an angel talking to her and now a baby! Of all things to say that an angel had even appeared to a woman, and in all places, Nazareth. I thought maybe she had gone mad. That was better than the alternative. But she did not act crazy. She acted perfectly sane. I could not focus on anything. I was a wreck. And the things people said! I had more than one person tell me to have her stoned! But I knew I still loved her."

"One day I came to the decided that I would send her quietly away. We would be divorced of the betrothal, and she would stay at her father's home. I, at least, hoped her father would keep her. She would probably be locked away for most of her life, and I honestly hoped she was crazy. In the morning I would go to her father's home and finalize the details. By this time we should have been married. But that night the last thing I could ever have expected, happened. An angel came to me in a dream, but I think Mary already told you this," he said.

Judah nodded. So Joseph continued, "I can't describe to you the dream, but it was very powerful." He paused again in remembering it. "In the morning I did go to Mary's father's house but with a very different plan in mind. After talking to Mary, I talked to her parents and told them that I wanted to take Mary home as my wife. They were both very surprised, and I could tell they wanted to ask me if the baby really was mine. I told them it was not, and then I told them about the dream. To this day I don't know if they believe either of us. I took Mary home with me that day as my wife. We have never been formally married with the big party and all, but we did the necessary steps so now we are husband and wife." Joseph smiled and looked over at Judah. "Does that satisfy your curiosity?"

"Oh, yes Sir, thank you Sir," Judah responded. Joseph raised an eyebrow and looked at him. Judah paused, "I mean Joseph."

"That's better," smiled Joseph. "Now I am going to go to sleep too." And with that he lay down beside Mary and soon fell asleep.

Judah crawled into his corner again, but sleep did not come. Not for several hours at least. There was far too much on his mind. Could God really care? Had He not abandoned them like Judah thought? Judah remembered sitting at his father's feet and following his mother around when he was little. They had told him stories of Israel's history. Stories of Abraham, Isaac, Jacob, and Joseph, the slavery in Egypt, and God's deliverers through Moses. Stories of how they had conquered the land with Joshua, how when the people turned back to God they were delivered by a judge. He always loved hearing about King David and all the good that was done through his reign. His parents had always talked of the promise of the Messiah. He would be of the line of David.

The prophets had promised his coming. God had not forgotten His people but would send them a deliverer. Judah had soaked in everything they had said when he was little. He had believed every word, but no more.

Judah no longer believed God cared. How could he? Judah's parents were gone. They had died with the rest of his family. It was only Hadassah and he left. He had looked at the facts. God had not spoken to any prophets in hundreds of years. There was no word from God. There had even been word from God in the Babylonian captivity. They had come back, gotten things straightened out, and then God stopped talking. There was still no Messiah and no king on the throne from the line of David. Rather they had a king set up by Rome, and the emperor in Rome controlled everything. This census proved that. But he had decided that God did not care, at least for the common people, when his family died. Almost everyone in his village had died, all his friends and everyone that mattered.

He had Hadassah, who was his only comfort, but he had to be the big brother now. He had to be strong for her now. The day his family died, something else died in him. He had not cried again. As for God being a loving God, who would send someone to save them in the form of the Messiah, he no longer believed that. He had stopped believing that a long time ago.

But today, today all of that had been challenged. Everything Mary and Joseph had said seemed to contradict that. An angel showing up to people! He could see one showing up to a priest, but to common people just like him? They were barely old enough to be considered adults. Why would God send angels to them? And the message they brought! Why it sounded like this child was more than just a child, or even special, but the MESSIAH!!! Could it be that God was keeping His word, and He really did care? Judah closed his eyes.

"God, I don't know if I can talk to you like this," he prayed. "I am sorry if You really do care. I don't know if I'm right or wrong. Could You help me understand?" Judah had not felt this confused in a long time, but part of him, deep down inside, was daring to hope, that just maybe God did care.

Judah slept fitfully that night, and morning seemed to come way too soon. But, Judah made himself get up and start the day.

The morning was busy and although he tried to stay with Mary as much as possible, he had other things to do. Samuel kept him busy and for a time he had to concentrate on the things at hand. He shoved all other thoughts to the back of his mind, which he was so good at doing. In the afternoon he was released to work on some things in the stable where he would be out of the way, and he could watch Mary. He had not been there long when he noticed Mary seemed uncomfortable. When he asked her how she was she said,

"Oh I'm fine, I think." She paused for a little then turned to Judah again. "I did all the talking yesterday, now it is your turn."

"Oh, I don't have anything that interesting or important to say," he replied.

She smiled. "Have you always lived in Bethlehem?" she asked.

"No, Hadassah and I have lived with Samuel for," he paused, "over a year now."

"Is Samuel family?" she asked.

"He's a distant relative."

"Where does the rest of your family live?"

Judah took a deep breath and answered slowly. "We all lived in a small village north of here."

"May I ask what happened?"

"A disease broke out. No one really knows what caused it. Some said it was the water, others said something else. I even heard someone say that God must have been mad at us."

"Do you have any other family members still alive?"

Judah looked over at her and saw only genuine care and concern on her face.

"One of my little sisters lived. Her name is Hadassah. She works in the kitchen most times with Martha, the cook." He paused and looked up at Mary again. "You remind me of my older sister Abigail in some ways. She was about your age and engaged too. She was so sweet. She always looked out for us younger children. She was excited to be betrothed to Jacob. She would have been a good mother." He paused again. A lump welled up in his throat. He looked over at Mary, "I haven't talked about this with anyone ever," he said. Mary patted the ground beside her, and he came and sat down.

"How about you tell me about it, if you want to?" she said.

He had not wanted to talk about this for a long time, but now it felt like he needed to talk, or he would burst. "The old and the young got sick first. It wasn't just our family, but everyone in the village. How Hadassah and I never got sick, I don't know. Abigail worked along side Mother to take care of everyone. She kept Hadassah and me away from all the others who were sick. She worked so hard, and when Mother and Father got sick, she took care of them too. Then…" He took in another ragged breath and continued. "She got sick. There was no one left to take care of her. I tried to but she wouldn't let me. She kept saying she was fine, and I would believe her, but I knew deep down inside she wasn't. Then one morning I went in to check on her, and she was dead. I hadn't had the heart to tell her that the day before, Jacob had died. Maybe I could have taken care of her better. If I had just done more, I could have kept her from dying, and everyone else too, like Mother and Father, and my other brothers and sisters. There were seven of us. I kept Hadassah away, but maybe I could have done more. I could have done more! Why did God let this happen?!" Judah cried. For the first time in a long time, Judah felt hot tears running down his face. Mary leaned over and put her arms around him and held him close.

"Judah, I don't know if you could have done anything more for your family, but I doubt it. And even though we don't know each other very well, I think I have seen enough of you to know you did everything you could. You are a very brave boy. And Judah," she said, lifting his chin up so she could look him in the face, "no matter what you think, God has not abandoned us. He still cares for His people. You'll see. Maybe that's what this baby, and Joseph and I, can teach you. I know God still cares," she reassured him. She just held him then, and he held onto her as he let the tears fall. No words were spoken, but none needed to be. Finally he lifted his head, and Mary began to wipe away his tears. He reached up his own hand and swiped them away, and then he said in a shaky voice,

"I haven't cried since then. I just held it all inside, I guess, and told myself that I would never cry again, and that I was too big for that."

Mary smiled and nodded as she reached up to wipe away a tear from her own eye. "It's not bad or wrong to cry. Sometimes we just need to let it out." She smiled again. "Even boys," she said as she gave him a squeeze.

They sat there next to each other for a while. Judah amazingly felt relieved. He knew he could not have picked a better person to share all this with. He had not realized how much it had all been bottled up inside until he started to let it out, and once it had started to come out, he could not stop it.

Judah was startled when he felt someone shaking his shoulder. He opened his eyes to Mary gently shaking him. He was surprised to realize he had fallen asleep.

"Judah," she said, "wake up."

"What is it Mary?" he asked casually.

"I don't mean to alarm you but…" she trailed off. She had his full attention now. "I think the baby is coming," she said gently.

If he wasn't fully awake before, he was for sure now. "The Baby!" he shouted. "Uh, um, I'll go get someone!" he said, and with that he was on his feet, and running for the upper part of the house. He ran up the stairs and through the door and on through the house. He was not even sure who he was looking for, but when he found Samuel and Martha talking he figured if anyone would do, these would be the people to tell. "Samuel, Samuel!" he yelled as he ran up to them.

"Goodness boy, what are you yelling for?" Samuel said turning to Judah. But when he saw Judah's face his own expression changed. "What is wrong Judah?" he asked.

"Mary…the lady…down…in the stable area," he said, gasping between breaths.

"Yes. What about her?" Samuel asked.

"The Baby! It's coming!" Judah blurted out.

The Guests in the Stable

Samuel's eyebrows rose in surprise, but it was Martha who spoke, bursting into action.

"You take me down to her right now," she demanded. "Hadassah!" she called over her shoulder to Judah's little sister who was standing just a little way off, trying to sweep the floor amidst all the people. "I am going to need you too."

Judah hurried back down to the stable with Martha right beside him and Hadassah behind her. Mary was bent over in pain when they arrived.

"How long have they been coming?" Martha asked as she hurried to Mary's side.

"Most of the afternoon," Mary replied. "I was not sure at first, but they keep coming harder and faster."

Judah was not sure what she was talking about, but Martha seemed to know. She started to help Mary lie down and get into a more comfortable position.

Mary turned to Judah and asked, "Can you please go find Joseph for me?"

Judah nodded and hurried away. He was not sure how he was going to find him, but he was sure going to try. He ran out into the street and looked around, then started running down the street searching faces hoping to see Joseph. There were so many people he had to push his way through and the noise was still deafening. Time seemed to crawl, and Judah felt more and more frantic. Finally, through the crowd, he spotted Joseph's face. Joseph looked tired and weary as he walked along.

"Joseph!" Judah yelled, pushing through the crowd to reach him. Joseph lifted up his head, having heard his name called, and when he saw Judah running through the crowd toward him, his face took on a look of worry.

"What is it Judah?" he asked as soon as Judah reached him.

"It's Mary. The baby's coming!"

Judah saw the fear jump into Joseph's eyes. He started hurrying down the street so fast, Judah had to run to keep up with him. When they reached the house, Judah was exhausted, but he ran in after

Joseph. Mary was lying on the floor, and Martha and Hadassah were trying to make her comfortable, but she looked like she was in pain. Joseph hurried to her side and held her hand.

"When I saw Judah, I knew something was wrong," he said.

"It's okay Joseph," she replied. "I will be fine; it's just time."

"And it is time for you boys to leave," said Martha trying to hurry them out.

"But," protested Joseph.

"No buts," Martha replied. "You boys should not be in here. Now go outside. If I need anything, I will let you know." And with that, she shooed them outside.

Joseph sat down outside, and Judah thought he looked like he could cry. Judah sat down beside him, not sure what else to do. Neither one spoke, for there was nothing to say. Judah felt like he should break the silence, but he could think of nothing good to say. He wondered if Joseph would even listen. He was soon caught up in listening to what was going on inside. Every time a noise came from inside the stable both of them would almost jump. Time tricked by, and night began to fall. Judah was caught up in his own thoughts when Joseph suddenly stood up. Judah looked up to see Hadassah standing in the entryway of the stable.

"What is it?" Judah asked quickly hurrying over to her about the same time that Joseph did.

"Martha wants a bucket of water," she said holding out a bucket. "She also says everything is fine," Hadassah told them.

Judah took the bucket. "I'll go," he said.

With the bucket in hand, he raced off down the street to the well. There were still a few people on the street, but most were gone. By now it was dark, and the stars were starting to come out. When he reached the well, he quickly filled the bucket and ran back down the street, slopping water as he went. When he reached the stable Hadassah hurried out to meet him and took the bucket.

"I can carry it," he offered.

Hadassah shook her head. "Martha will not allow it," she replied as she walked back in carrying the bucket.

The Guests in the Stable

Slowly he sat back own beside Joseph and started waiting again. The night dragged on as they waited. The silence of the night was cut every so often by a cry or moan from Mary inside the stable. Every time she cried out, Joseph would jump and look. He would get up and pace, then sit back down, then get up again. Judah understood his jumpiness. He felt it too. He remembered his mother having babies, but most times he and the others were hurried off to a friend or family's house in town. When they came back, there would be a new baby. But this time was different. He was older now and understood more. He also knew that women often died giving birth to babies.

But even so, this was different. Mary was special. She did remind him of his sister, but her story had touched him too. This baby was bound to be special. Joseph, Mary, and even this unborn baby had touched him deep inside. They represented a new life and a new beginning. But, there was more than that. He couldn't quite put his finger on it or understand it. He thought long and hard. He could not sleep anyway. He went back over everything they had told him. The angel and his message of hope, and now, everything that was happening. Could it be that maybe, just maybe, God did care? Care for more then those in high positions, who did all the right things at just the right times? Maybe God did care for the common people too. And maybe, just maybe, He cared about one little orphan boy who lived in the little town of Bethlehem with old Samuel. The very thought practically knocked all the air right out of him. If God could care about him, then He must not have forgotten about His people or have left them. The more Judah thought about it the more he was sure it was true. An angel had come to Mary and Joseph to tell them about this baby. This Baby. Yes, this baby seemed to be more too. Angels had appeared to other women to tell them about their babies, and they always ended up being great people. Could this baby become the great person they had all been waiting for? Could this baby be the, Messiah?

His thoughts were interrupted then by the sound of a baby's cry. He looked at Joseph, and Joseph looked at him, then they were both on their feet running into the stable. When they were inside, they both stopped when everyone looked up at them. Martha was wrapping the baby in a cloth, and Hadassah was helping Mary into a sitting position.

After Martha finished wrapping the baby, she placed him in Mary's arms. Mary looked down at the baby and, smiling, gave a sigh of relief as she ran her finger over the baby's face. Looking up again, she smiled at Joseph and waved him over saying,

"Come meet your son, Joseph." Joseph walked up slowly and sat down beside Mary. He placed his arm around her, and she laid her head on his shoulder. Judah pulled back into the shadows of the doorway. Maybe he should not be here.

Mary slowly lifted her head and looked at Joseph. "Do you want to hold him?" she asked.

Joseph was silent and looked lost for words, so Mary lifted the little bundle and placed it in his arms. At first he did not move, but then he shifted the bundle to one arm and laid his other hand on the baby's head. "His name will be Jesus," he said, "Just as we were told." Then he placed his arm back around Mary, and she placed her head back on his shoulder.

After Martha finished washing her hands in the bucket, she turned to Mary and Joseph and said, "Hadassah and I are going back upstairs, but if you need anything at all, you just send Judah for me, and I will be down right away." And with that, she picked up the bucket in one hand and took Hadassah's hand in the other and walked out.

"All right, and thank you," Mary called out as they left. Then she looked directly at Judah and smiled. "You can come over here, Judah," she invited.

Judah hesitated, not sure if he should or not.

"It's okay, Judah, come meet Jesus," Joseph said, waving him over.

Judah slowly walked up and knelt down in the hay in front of them. Joseph lifted the little baby and handed him back to Mary. The baby squirmed and started to whimper, then went into a full out scream.

"I think I need to feed him," Mary said.

Judah scrambled back to his feet and turned away feeling awkward.

The Guests in the Stable

"I wonder where we are going to put him. I suppose he could sleep between us, but I am not sure that is the best idea," Joseph said almost like he was thinking aloud.

Judah looked around, trying to think of something they could lay the baby in. Then he spotted it, a small manger off to the side of one of the stalls.

"How about this?" He asked running over to it. "I could fill it with nice hay and there's an old bag that we used to put grain in that is empty now. I could put that on top so the hay does not make him itchy."

Joseph smiled and nodded. Judah hurried over to the manger and emptied it of all the old hay and grain, then he hurried about to get some nice hay, then off to find the grain sack. By the time it was all ready and in place, Mary was done nursing and baby Jesus was sound asleep in her arms. Joseph carried the manger over beside Mary and sat it down, and then he sat down beside her again. Judah seated himself at their feet.

"Isn't our son perfect," Mary whispered as she stroked his head again. Joseph smiled, but then a sad look came across his face.

"He's not really my son," he said.

"Yes he is, Joseph," Mary replied. "God chose you to be his father. I am not sure who his father is, I guess God Himself, but he needs a father here on earth, and God could not have picked a better man."

Joseph smiled again and placed a kiss on her forehead. "And God could not have picked a better mother."

Judah watched all of this and felt out of place. This was for them, and he felt like an intruder. But he did not have much time to dwell on that because Mary turned to him and asked, "Would you like to hold him?" Judah froze not sure what to say. Joseph must have seen the fear and surprise in his eyes.

"It's okay Judah, he will not fall apart in your arms. You can hold him."

With Judah sitting at their feet, Mary just leaned forward and placed the baby in his arms. At first Judah was stiff; it had been a while since he had held a baby, but the baby stirred only slightly as he nestled himself deep in Judah's arms. Judah felt his spirit rise like it had not in years. This little baby did not look any different than any other baby, but Judah knew deep down that this was no ordinary baby. Everything had happened just as the angel had said it would, and it was not what Mary or Joseph could have predicted. This baby was special. Somehow, Judah knew that this baby would be the Messiah. But he had another feeling he could not quite explain. It was like there was more, that this little baby in his arms was more then the Messiah. Judah could not explain it, and he did not say anything, but he knew that this baby was very special and the world would probably never be the same.

Judah just held the baby Jesus for a long time, and then he handed him back to Mary, who laid him in the neat, little, manger bed he had made. It was late, and he knew he should try to get some sleep, but he knew there would be no sleep tonight.

That is when he heard the noise at the door. Judah got to his feet and looked over to see several scraggly looking shepherds come through the door. They only seemed to have eyes for the baby. They slowly walked in, and he could see awestruck wonder in their eyes. Judah hurried to ask what they were doing there. They explained how they had been told by angels about the birth and how they had come looking for this baby.

The shepherds gathered around, and Mary let each of them hold the baby. Judah noticed a boy about his own age hanging back. He looked awestruck, and his eyes were full of wonder. Judah knew just how he felt. The night slipped away and the shepherds left just before dawn. Judah could hear them singing psalms of praise and telling everyone they met of their strange encounter and all that had happened and that God had spoken once more. Judah felt just as joyful as they did.

As dawn came and he could hear the house starting to come to life above them, he helped Mary and Joseph settled in, then he offered to get them some food from the kitchen. They agreed, but before he even left, he saw they had pretty much fallen asleep in each other's arms. Judah slipped out of the stable and up the stairs and into the house, then back to the kitchen. Even though the sun was not quite up yet, people were up and about and the noise was rising quickly. But for once Judah did not care. Nothing could dampen his mood. He walked into the kitchen and sat down on a small bench most times used as a stepping stool. At that moment Hadassah walked in.

"You look exhausted!" she said.

"Yea," he nodded then smiled.

She looked back at him then exclaimed, "You're smiling! I mean I have not seen you smile like that in a long time."

Judah nodded and he felt his smile get bigger. "Come here," he said, and when she did, he wrapped her in a big hug. "I plan to do a lot more smiling now," he said.

"Really!" she squealed.

"Yup, you see, I learned some very important things recently."

"Like what?" Hadassah questioned.

"Like God has not forgotten His people, and He still cares for us, even me and you sister." Judah pulled her back and looked deep into her eyes. "I don't want you to ever forget that, okay?" he said.

"I won't," she said. "I promise."

A Shepherd Tale

Benjamin opened his eyes and stared up at the dark ceiling. What was the point in trying to sleep anymore? He was wide awake, as he had been most of the night. He listened intently to see if he could hear anyone. Maybe the feet of someone coming to wake him? But there was no one. All was quiet and still. "Still as a tomb," he thought. Tombs. The thought made him shutter. Two weeks earlier they had placed his father in a tomb. There were those, however, who said his father should not even have that honor. But his father had come from a prominent family and so his body had not been thrown in a pit or trench somewhere, like most common criminals. But in a way his father had not been a common criminal. He had been worse.

Benjamin's family, including his father, was from the tribe of Levi, the priestly tribe, and their family was from the line of priests. His father had been in charge of the temple treasury. That was how he had gotten in trouble. He had been caught stealing temple money. In fact, it came out that he had been stealing temple money for a long time. Benjamin and his mother were horrified; they had no idea he had been doing this. He had been caught and put on trial and judged by the Sanhedrin, whom he had been a part of. They found him guilty and sentenced him to death. They then took him outside the city and stoned him to death, then and there. Benjamin turned over and started crying again. That seemed to be the only thing he could do these days. He could be thankful that he had not had to witness his father's death. His uncle (his father's brother) had come to tell him and his poor mother. But that was the only thing he could be thankful for, he felt. His father, from a fine priestly family, a Sadducee, and well respected, had been caught stealing, stealing from the temple treasury no less. That which he was suppose to watch over and be in charge of. He then was condemned by men who were his friends and put to death by those same men.

His father's brother, Uncle Asher, had taken them in then. It was just Benjamin and his mother. She had never been able to have any more children. Benjamin had grown up having all of his parent's love to himself. He had always wanted and planned to be just like his father, and one day maybe even being in charge of the temple treasury himself. Now all of those dreams and plans had been shattered. They would never allow the son of a thief to be in charge of the temple treasury, even though he had done nothing wrong, Benjamin knew he would forever be punished for his father's crime.

Benjamin continued to let the hot tears fall. Some would have scolded him for crying. A boy of twelve did not cry, but Benjamin did not care anymore what they would say. He had already heard next to everything that could be said about his father and his family. He cried for all that had happened, for all that had been lost, and for the future. Maybe that was the worst part of it all. Benjamin and his Uncle Asher had never gotten along very well. His father said that Uncle Asher was jealous of his father being the oldest and all they had had. His uncle now seemed half proud that they had lost everything and their name was run into the dirt. But all around, Benjamin thought that none of them were very happy that they now had to depend on him. But as his uncle had said, they would have to make the best of it. His mother could live with them permanently. And Benjamin? Well, for one, all schooling would end, and Benjamin knew that with that went any chance of further learning and one day becoming a Sadducee and a member of the Sanhedrin, just like his father. No, Benjamin could no longer be like his father, even in the good things his father had been.

No, his uncle had decided a much better life for him. He was to go and help tend his uncle's sheep. He was to be a shepherd. A Shepherd! Shepherds were the lowest of people, smelly, dirty, and unkempt. Benjamin had made jokes about shepherds with his friends before. Now he was to be one. His life plans went from being a member of the great Counsel, to a filthy shepherd. This, too, seemed like a slap in the face and a punishment he must suffer for his father's crimes. Yes, one more thing that was his father's fault. But in it all Benjamin could not decide if he hated his father for all of this or if he was just sorry for his death and the loss of all that Benjamin had had.

Benjamin's father had been his hero and idol. Benjamin had more than wanted to be just like his father. He had wanted his father to be proud of him and pleased in all he did. And that had not been easy. His father had been a tough man and not easy to please. You had to be and do it all perfectly. And that would often just keep you out of trouble. To get his attention and approval was all but impossible, but Benjamin had never stopped trying. Once in a great while he had, but those times were so few that Benjamin could hardly remember them. His father had become increasingly distant in the past few years. Looking back on it, that may have been to try and hide what he was doing.

Benjamin wiped away his tears and rolled over to look up at the dark ceiling again. Never would he please his father again. Instead he would have to become a shepherd, a profession his father had detested. But there was nothing that could be done about it. Benjamin and his mother were now dependent on Uncle Asher, and if Uncle Asher wanted Benjamin to tend his sheep, that is what Benjamin would have to do.

Benjamin lay still and waited. More of the same kind of thoughts swirled through his head. He had half fallen back to sleep when he heard footsteps. They stopped outside the doorway. His uncle's head peeked in.

"Benjamin," he half snapped in the darkness, "time to get up." Now came the time that all Benjamin knew would end, and in many ways, it felt like his life was ending too. But there was nothing to be done about it, so he rolled himself over and sat up.

Benjamin looked down at the clothes that had been laid out for him. They were new to him, but they did not look like clothes that he would describe or think of as new. He reached down and picked up the rough thick, outer tunic. He slipped it on over his head then reached for the other object. It was a sheep skin mantel. This was a new clothing item to him, but he knew it was normal and useful to a shepherd. It would keep him warm and would be used like a blanket at night to wrap up in. Last came his sandals. He put those on and straightened up. He took one last look around the room that had been his bedroom for the past two weeks. He looked down at his cousin on the other end of the room. His cousin lay sound asleep with a blanket over his head, and Benjamin knew he would be furious if he woke him to say goodbye. Even though they were close in age, his cousin being a year younger, they were not close as friends. His cousin had made it clear he felt no pity for Benjamin about what had happened to Benjamin's father. Rather he had puffed himself up since Benjamin and his mother came to live with them. Benjamin sighed. His aunt had not been much better, and he hated to have to leave his mother here with them, but there was nothing he could do about it. With one last look, Benjamin turned and left the room.

Benjamin walked down the hall to the main room. One lamp lit the room and cast the three figures there in shadows. One was his Uncle Asher looking as impatient as ever. The second was his poor mother who was close to tears. The third was a stranger Benjamin had never seen. The stranger was of normal height, maybe a little shorter. His face was so brown and covered in wrinkles that Benjamin could not make out what his expression was. The shadows dancing around the room hid the stranger further. But his clothes told Benjamin what he needed to know. His dress was the same as Benjamin's which meant this man must be the shepherd who would lead him to the flock and teach him everything he needed to know. Benjamin hoped he could make friends with this haggard old man.

"Really Benjamin? How long does it take for you to get dressed? You have a long walk before you get to the flock, and the sooner you get started the better," snapped Uncle Asher.

To Benjamin's surprise the old shepherd spoke, "There is no need to be in a big hurry." Uncle Asher turned and scowled at the old man, but the old shepherd's wrinkled face did not change. Benjamin was surprised and impressed. Most men cowered under his uncle's scowl and did not talk back, but the old man did not seem to care or even acknowledge that his uncle was glaring at him.

His mother stepped forward, and as she handed him a purse-like pouch she spoke in a shaky voice. "Here," she said, "I packed some food that should last you for a while, and this," she added handing him a water-skin. Benjamin slipped them over his head and shoulder and let them fall by his side.

"Thanks Ma," he sputtered back as his voice started to shake as well. His mother tried to give him a smile as she stepped closer to hug him. She slipped her arms around him and in return Benjamin put his around her and clung to her. He could feel two hot tears slip down his cheeks and from his mother's shaking shoulders he knew she was crying too. Benjamin felt like a little helpless boy again in his mother's arms.

"I love you," she whispered in his ear.

"I love you too, Ma," he choked back.

Uncle Asher cleared his throat loudly. "You need to be going now Benjamin," he said. Benjamin could hear the irritation in his voice. His mother pulled back and put both of her shaking hands on his face. Her eyes were full of tears and her checks were all wet.

"Be a good boy, Benjamin," she said.

"I will, Ma," Benjamin promised in a shaking voice as he nodded and raised a hand to wipe his face. He then turned and followed the old shepherd outside the house. It was still dark with faint hints of the sun coming up in the East. It was also cold. As they walked down the street Benjamin looked back at the house. His Uncle Asher stood leaning against the door frame with his hands crossed in front of him. He looked like he always had in Benjamin's mind, hard and half-disappointed in or about something. His mother was also standing there. She looked small and alone, and Benjamin had to fight the urge to run back to her. She tried to smile and raised her hand to wave at him. Benjamin waved back. He then looked over his shoulder and saw that the shepherd was a good ways ahead of him. He gave one quick last wave and ran to catch up. His mother dropped her hand to her mouth as she watched her only child and son disappear down the street.

Benjamin focused on following and keeping up with the shepherd. As they walked through the streets Benjamin realized he did not even know the man's name. Oh well, he would find out soon. At first they walked through streets that Benjamin knew. He had not lived far from his Uncle, though they had rarely visited each other. They were heading to Gennath Gate which was one of the city gates. They had to travel north to get to the Gennath Gate because the road that led to Bethlehem and Hebron was from this gate. Benjamin knew that his Uncle Asher's flock was kept on the hills around Bethlehem. The walk had warmed him some, but he was now thankful for the mantel he was wearing. He turned to look at the shepherd who was walking slowly with his staff.

"What is your name," Benjamin asked.

"Seth," the old shepherd replied.

"My name is Benjamin," Benjamin said without thinking.

"I know," Seth replied half smiling.

Benjamin felt a little foolish after that. "Of course he knows who I am," he thought. The sun was climbing toward the surface, although it was still on the other side of the city. There were not many people traveling their way to the city gate. Most people would want to be coming into the city in the morning, not leaving. As they walked Benjamin caught site of a few Roman soldiers here and there. They were a constant reminder that Judea was not a free county anymore. Finally they reached the gate.

"Quick," Seth motioned as he went on ahead. There were a lot of people wanting to get into the city, so they had to work their way through the crowds to get out. There was a time or two when Benjamin lost sight of Seth, but he would always find him again in a few seconds. In time they got to a place where they could slip off the main road and get out of the crowd. They were barely out of the crowd when Benjamin heard a voice cut through the noise,

"What are those filthy shepherds doing here? They should be out on the hills, not here around decent people." There was a slight murmur of agreement, and Benjamin saw eyes narrow as they looked at him. He felt angry for a moment, and then he felt shame. How many times had he thought and said such words, if not worse. He had never thought he would be on this side of things. He hung his head in shame. He was surprised when he felt a hand fall on his shoulder. He looked up right into Seth's old, kind eyes.

"Never mind them, son," he said giving another half smile.

First they traveled west around the city walls, then they turned south as the walls and road turned down toward Bethlehem. First they passed Herod's palace that was now nearly finished. As the morning grew warmer they continued to travel down and away from Jerusalem. The rising sun and walking warmed Benjamin back up. He nibbled on a small cake of bread his mother had packed for him. He offered some to Seth who thanked him and took what he offered. They continued on in silence most of the morning. Shortly before they got to Bethlehem, Seth turned off the main road and walked up a hill where there was no road. Benjamin followed. They walked up and down several hills, passing another flock along the way. A shepherd called out and waved to Seth. Seth returned the gesture and they kept walking. They climbed a hill and found a large flock of sheep down the other side. One of the two men who were with the flock immediately walked over to them. Benjamin recognized him as one of his Uncle Asher's many servants. Seth spoke to the man. "You may now return to your master's house," he said. The man nodded and quickly walked away from them in the direction they had just come. Benjamin realized he must have been sent to find Seth and stay with the flock while Seth was gone. Seth chuckled as the servant left.

"He never much liked being a shepherd," he said. The other man more slowly approached them. He wore the same kind of dress as Seth and Benjamin, which identified him as a normal shepherd. He was young and some people would not have considered him to be a man yet. He was lean and tall and his skin was tan from long hours in the sun. Benjamin thought he looked familiar and might be a cousin of his, but he was not sure. The other man looked Benjamin up and down then turned to speak to Seth. Benjamin was not sure if this man approved of him or not.

"He is a terrible shepherd. Always complaining and never wanting to do any work. I guess he doesn't have to work too hard in that big house of Asher's," he remarked with disgust. Benjamin realized he was talking about the servant. He made a mental note to work hard and to try not to complain, at least not to this man. Seth turned to Benjamin.

"This is Ethan," he said.

"Pleased to meet you, Ethan," Benjamin said. Ethan seemed to look him over again then he nodded his acknowledgment. Seth seemed happier now and more comfortable. He smiled and his whole body seemed to relax.

"This is the flock we take care of. Before long you will know them all. Many even have names," remarked Seth to Benjamin as he waved his hand over all the sheep. Benjamin thought there seemed an awful lot of them to get to know them all.

"How many sheep are there?" he asked.

"Two hundred and twelve," Seth responded with pride. "About one hundred apiece."

"But not with me," remarked Benjamin when he had thought about it for a moment. Seth chuckled.

"No, you are not ready to be in charge of a hundred sheep yet. You are in training to take my place."

Benjamin was horrified. "Oh no! You see…well," Benjamin stuttered. "This is all wrong. Uncle Asher said he needed another shepherd. He didn't say anything about getting rid of one." Benjamin hung his head feeling terrible. Seth threw back his head and laughed.

"Oh, son," he said smiling at him. "I plan to stay with these sheep as long as I can, and if the good Lord permits, I will die right out here with them. But you see, I am getting old and it won't be long before I can't do all that I once could. You will be taking my place in all that, the hard work you see."

Benjamin felt better after this. He was not forcing anyone out of a job. That was good. But on the other hand he realized he would have to get used to working with Ethan. Maybe Ethan would soften up, and it would not be that bad. But if today was an indicator of how it would be, Benjamin was not looking forward to the future.

"We should be moving the sheep on," said Ethan, cutting into Benjamin's thoughts.

"Aye, that we should," agreed Seth.

For the next hour or so Benjamin was kept busy just walking and keeping up. As they walked some sheep ran ahead, seemingly knowing where they were going. Others lagged behind, but most just kept up and walked all around them. The sheep seemed to steer away from him, but they would travel close to Seth and Ethan, even rubbing legs with them and some almost getting under foot.

"You're still a stranger to them so they don't trust you yet," explained Seth. "But don't worry, before long they won't be afraid of you and will be all around you, too." They walked for about two miles before they stopped. Seth spent the next hour pointing out the different sheep to Benjamin. "Some of them have names, others do not. You soon get to know them all by their actions and personalities," Seth told Benjamin. Benjamin was feeling overwhelmed at all of this.

"How can you know all two hundred sheep?" he asked in bewilderment and amazement.

"Sheep have been a part of my life for nearly as long as I can remember. I have been with these sheep for years on end. They are my friends and family. Sometimes I can just feel it if one of them is missing. I can't explain it; it's just something you will learn with time," Seth told him.

Benjamin was disheartened. Time with the sheep was not what he wanted. If there was some way he could leave here, he would. But then again he may not be able to ever leave. The thought made him even sadder. And what if he did have to stay and could still not get it? What if he was a terrible shepherd! It was a job that all looked down on, but Benjamin had never thought about it being hard. What would people think of him if he could not do the least of jobs? He should not have to be a shepherd. He should be training to be in the temple. He should be studying the Torah, the law, not sheep faces and personalities.

"You all right son?" ask Seth interrupting his thoughts and bringing him back to the present. Embarrassed, Benjamin realized he had been glaring down at the sheep.

"Sorry, Seth, I just got lost in thought that's all," he muttered. To his surprise, Seth slapped him on the shoulder.

"That's just fine; we shepherds get plenty of time to think. That might be one of the things we are best at, thinking. You're already turning into a shepherd," Seth remarked with a laugh. Ethan looked back at them at this remark, and Benjamin half thought he seemed to sneer. Benjamin was not sure what to think. He knew Seth meant it as a compliment, but he did not want to be a shepherd. Oh, why did life have to be so mean?

After that Benjamin tried to keep his mind on whatever Seth was saying. They moved the sheep again later. By this time Benjamin was starving. He was used to sitting in a classroom, not trucking over the countryside. He ate from the purse his mother had sent with him. He noticed Seth and Ethan eating out of similar purses, but they were eating other things, things they would have gathered from the land. Once more Benjamin felt depressed. He would have to learn what could be eaten out here. Then get used to eating it. He liked his bed and "normal" food he thought. He must be the most unlucky boy in the world.

After they had eaten, they sort of lay down or sat against a rock and rested. Ethan and Seth even seemed to sleep, but Benjamin could not get comfortable. When he was just getting comfortable enough to maybe fall asleep, Ethan called to him.

"Hey kid, time to get these sheep moving again," he called. Benjamin forced himself to get up. The time spent lying down had given his body just enough time to start getting tight. He knew if he got moving again it would loosen back up, but, oh how he did not want to.

They walked farther this time than they had any time before. Benjamin wondered why and where they were going. They went down a narrow hill, and he found a stream running at the bottom. It was a little, shallow stream that the sheep were unafraid of and plunged right in. Benjamin was disappointed again. Once he had seen it he had hoped he might reach it before them and fill his skin with water. He had drunk most of it by now. But the sheep knew where they were going and had hurried down the hill right into the water to start drinking, stirring up mud and putting dirt into the water. Watering the sheep took longer than what Benjamin had realized. Seth and Ethan shifted the sheep through, making calls and grunts to get the sheep that were done drinking out and to let fresh sheep in. While the last of the sheep were getting a drink, Ethan and Seth moved upstream from them. Seth waved Benjamin to come along. When they were clear of the sheep and the muddy water they began to fill their skins. Benjamin now understood. They were likely nearly out of water too, but they took care of the sheep first, then they got their own water. Benjamin had much to learn, he realized, as he dropped his water skin into the water.

After watering the sheep, they trucked back the way they had come but in a little different direction. They walked a long way again but more slowly this time. Finally they stopped with a wide field below them. The sheep meandered down into the field to graze. The sun beat down on them in the heat of the day. Benjamin felt hot and tired. But Seth seemed to have ideas other then resting.

"Do you have a sling or a weapon of any kind on you, son?" he asked.

"No," Benjamin replied.

"Figured as much," Seth said. He fished into his purse bag. "Here," he said tossing him something. Benjamin managed to catch it before it hit him in the face. The thing turned out to be a sling. "You know how to use that?" he asked.

"Sort of, I think so," Benjamin replied. Seth nodded.

"Ethan over there," Seth said with a nod of his head in Ethan's direction. "He has a rod. It's shorter then my staff, and he carries it in his belt. It has a good knob on it and a few metal shards hammered into it. It can be used like a club. I have a sling too, but I am also handy with my staff here," Seth said patting it. "A sling is a good young man's weapon. I always carry some smooth rocks from the creek with me, but for practicing you might as well just use whatever small stones you can find."

First, Seth showed Benjamin what size stones to get, and then he showed him how to swing the sling. He explained that by swinging it overhead one could hit a cluster, but if one swung it at his side he could hit a hair on an animal's head. Seth then set Benjamin to work trying to use the sling.

"Throw the stones down the other side of the hill and away from the sheep," Seth said.

Ethan snorted. "He will not hit them. At least not on purpose, but I suppose it would not do to be scaring them ether," he said with a half laugh.

Benjamin tried, and tried, and tried some more but the more he tried, the more he thought it was hopeless. Seth would give him some advice now and then but for the most part he just watched. They moved the sheep again, but when they stopped, Seth sent him back to practicing again. The sun fell lower and lower in the sky. Finally Seth said that it was time to stop for the day. When Benjamin offered him back the sling, Seth told him to keep it; tomorrow he could practice some more. Benjamin did his best to keep the disappointment from his face.

They walked on for a time before they came to the top of a hill that opened up to a wide field. Benjamin stopped and looked down into the field. There were a large number of sheep down there already. Benjamin was a little surprised that they were headed down there too. Wouldn't the sheep all get mixed up? And, these other shepherds were there first. Would they get mad when other shepherds came down there too? However Seth, Ethan, and the sheep never paused. When they reached the bottom, four other shepherds walked up to them. "Good to see you again, Seth," the one greeted.

"I'm gone one night and you all miss me? Boy, I feel special," Seth teased back with a laugh.

"Well, maybe we just missed your reliability," the shepherd replied back. "Those hirelings can't be depended on to do anything, much less stay awake for a night watch. They wake up in the morning complaining how hard the good ground was and that they did not sleep a wink."

"But we all heard this one snoring," laughed one of the other young shepherds. Seth and the others joined in the laughter. Seth then pulled Benjamin forward.

"Friends," he said. "I would like you all to meet Benjamin. He is going to be working with Ethan and me from now on, and I am teaching him." Benjamin swallowed hard. Did they know who he was? Who his uncle was? Who his father was? Would they accept him or hate him? Much to his surprise and relief, all the other shepherds seemed friendly enough.

"Pleased to meet you, Benjamin," greeted the shepherd who had first spoken and the other shepherds chimed in.

Seth put his hand on Benjamin's shoulder, "We all spend the night together. It's more sheep but more of us too, and that makes watching them all at night easier," he explained. Seth then pointed to the first shepherd, "This is Amin," Seth said. Amin gave Benjamin a warm smile. Seth then turned to the second shepherd who had spoken and said, "This is Caleb." Seth then directed his attention to the last two shepherds. One was older then Seth and the other was closer to Ethan's age. "This is Eli," he said as he introduced the older man. "That young man is his grandson, Jeb."

"And here come Jethro and Jebal," said Amin as he pointed to the hills. Benjamin could see two more shepherds coming down the hill with about the same number of sheep that they had. This makes a lot of sheep Benjamin thought. Separating them in the morning will be impossible. When the last two shepherds came, Benjamin was introduced to them as well, and they to him. They were brothers. Jethro was the older one in his mid thirties and Jebal was in his late twenties. Amin was in his forties and Caleb his twenties.

Slowly all sat down and began pulling things from their bags to eat. Benjamin had not realized how hungry he had become until he started eating again. As he stuffed more of the food his mother had packed for him in his mouth, he looked around to see what the rest were eating. Mostly it was plants and things one would find out in the fields. Few had bread and such things, but most seemed to have dried meat of some kind. Night fell around them and Benjamin's eyes got very heavy. The others started to talk more though. Their conversations varied but often it was about Scripture and what it meant. Normally Benjamin would have loved to stay up and listen to the talk, but this night he was too tired. He was exhausted! He had gotten little sleep the night before, and all day had been spent trucking up and down hills and trying to learn how to use the sling. He just wanted to lie down and go to sleep.

Suddenly someone was shaking him. Benjamin opened his eyes and looked up right into Seth's face. He then realized he had fallen asleep.

Seth smiled down at him. "Come on," Seth said. Benjamin slowly got to his feet, amazed at how stiff he had become. His neck ached from his head hanging down on his chest and his back hurt from being hunched over. When he looked around he noticed that the others were getting up too. Some had already left. Seth saw him looking around.

"We form a circle around the sheep to protect them," Seth explained. "You will be with me," he added. They moved a ways out from where they had been. They passed Amin and walked on a ways before they stopped. Ethan walked past them. Everyone was spread out to the point that one could hardly see the other. They were just close enough however, that something could not get through without being seen or heard.

Benjamin lay down and curled himself up inside his mantel, very thankful for it now. He was not used to sleeping on the ground, but this night it did not matter. He had barely laid his head down and closed his eyes when he fell asleep.

Once more Benjamin felt himself being shaken awake. He tried to fight it this time. He moaned and rolled away from the hand that shook him.

"Benjamin," Seth called to him. "Wake up."

Benjamin forced one eye open. All was dark. "It can't be morning," he mumbled.

Seth chuckled and responded, "No it is not morning."

"Then let me sleep," Benjamin snapped back.

"We have the second watch," Seth said. "You have to get up and help me." Unwillingly Benjamin forced his eyes open and looked up at Seth.

"What do you mean exactly?" he inquired.

"We all have a watch. The night is split into seven watches. Eli and Jeb share the last watch. Amin starts and it goes around the circle like that. When our watch is done, we wake Ethan just as Amin woke me."

"How do we know when our watch is done?" asked Benjamin.

"Oh, you learn to know it by the stars and moon. Also your body gets used to being awake for this time period," Seth reassured him. At this moment Benjamin did not feel too sure about that. But again he did not feel too sure about anything. He just wanted to cry, but he was too tired for that too.

Then Benjamin remembered something. "Isn't the night split into four watches?" he asked.

"Most times it is," answered Seth. "But we split it up among all of us. It gives everyone a turn and everyone more time to sleep. We all have to be up all day too."

He sat by Seth and tried his hardest to stay awake. Seth told him what to watch for in the sheep to know if something was wrong. Seth said lots of things to him, but he rarely answered. He was just too tired for talking. After what seemed like an eternity and Seth repeatedly having to push him or shake him to keep him awake, Seth said their watch was done. He got up and walked away to wake Ethan. Benjamin knew he should stay awake until Seth got back, but he couldn't remember if he did or not. The next thing he remembered was Seth shaking him and telling him it was morning. Benjamin opened his eyes and looked up. The sky was starting to get light in the East. It was morning this time.

He tried to sit up and get to his feet, but he found that his muscles had tightened in his sleep. They all but refused to move now. Benjamin almost cried out in pain as he slowly moved. He had never in his life been this sore. When he did get to his feet, he looked around to find he was the last to get up. All the others were busy moving and hurrying about. Soon all the shepherds had split up into each of their groups. After that the shepherds all began calling or whistling out to the sheep. As they did this they all walked away in different directions. To Benjamin's amazement all the sheep began to split up into their groups as well. There was no one among them, driving them apart. They were all following their own shepherd's voice. As the shepherds walked away all the sheep followed. Not one was left standing, unsure of where to go.

"Seth, how does that work?" asked Benjamin in amazement.

Seth smiled. "All the sheep know their own shepherd's voice. They will not follow a stranger. From now on whenever we start calling them, you should too. Have your own call; make one up if you need to," said Seth.

As they walked away Benjamin tried a few different calls and such, but in the end he was not sure what to call. They walked away and after a time came to a place Benjamin recognized as close to where Seth and he had found them the morning before. Benjamin sighed. They were back to the beginning again in a way.

The day slipped by much as the last had been. The same areas were gone to and the same things were done. Night came and went as the last had and so in this way a week past. At the end of it, Benjamin was surprised at just how much he had learned. Not only how much he had learned, but how much he had changed. He felt stronger and not so foolish out here. That was not to say he felt equal in abilities to the other shepherds. He felt less of the boy who lived a cushy life in the city, sitting in a room and listening to rabbis all day, and more of the hardened shepherd who could sleep on the ground, keep his watch without falling asleep, and get up in the morning refreshed. He was finally getting the hang of the sling and just how to use it. As he sat around with the other shepherds this night he did not feel so tired.

He had long run out of his own food and was eating the same things the others were eating. He tried not to think about what he was eating and just get it down. After they finish eating, Benjamin stayed sitting where he was. Most nights he had gotten up and gone to where he and Seth would sleep, and got a few more winks. Tonight he decided to stay and hear what they talked about. Ethan and Jeb were sitting together and seemed to be having their own private conversation. Everyone else seemed to be a part of the other conversation. The topics varied from sheep and what had happened that day to what they heard was going on in Bethlehem and Jerusalem. They were closer to Bethlehem than Jerusalem, but Bethlehem was just a small town and most things took place in Jerusalem, at least anything worth hearing about.

"So Eli," Caleb asked, "any more word if that nephew of yours is going to keep the sheep or if he really has decided to sell them?"

"I have not heard any more about him selling the sheep. But I doubt he will sell all of them yet."

"Why you say that?" inquired Seth.

A Shepherd Tale

"I don't think he wants this smelly old shepherd invading his nice clean house in Jerusalem," Eli replied with a laugh. The others joined in laughing. Benjamin had learned that because most people looked down on the shepherds, the shepherds did not think too highly of them either and made fun of them being so picky and clean. "No, I don't think he will get rid of all the sheep until I drop dead," Eli stated.

"Then they will have me to deal with," remarked Jeb from the side. He had apparently been listening in.

"Yes, but you are young, and they will find something for you. That or just throw you out. I am too old for them to do that respectfully. Ah, I pity you my lad. Your life is still young and new, and full of uncertainty. But I, I am old. My life will soon be done. I tell you all I look forward to the day I die and my soul departs this old, body and goes to the hereafter, or wherever it goes, to be with the Lord I think," said Eli.

Seth gave a strong sound of agreement from where he sat beside Benjamin. All the others nodded or gave a grunt of agreement. Benjamin was a little surprised. He had always been taught there was no soul. When one died, you were dead, no more, no after life, no nothing like that. This life and all you have in it, was all the reward one would ever get.

The conversation continued on but Benjamin's thoughts often returned to this. Did Seth agree with all that Eli had said? Did he think more like a Pharisee? Benjamin's father was a Sadducee and so that was how he had been raised. It would seem this was not the same for Seth. The more Benjamin thought about it, the more he realized that it was likely Seth would not agree with the Sadducees beliefs. Sadducees were of priestly blood of highly important families. The Pharisees were more popular with the common people. Shepherds were with that group, not with the noble, high, or priestly.

Time slipped by and the conversation died. All slowly got up and went to their guard/sleeping place and went to sleep. Benjamin did get some sleep before Seth woke him to help keep watch. Benjamin had found that talking with Seth helped to keep him awake for the watch, but tonight he was still thinking about things from earlier and did not talk much.

"You okay?" Seth asked.

"Huh? Oh yea, why?" Benjamin replied dragging himself back to the present.

"Because you have been awfully quite and did not respond when I asked you a question," Seth told him with a smile.

Benjamin felt a little embarrassed but gave Seth a smile back. "I have just been thinking," he told Seth.

"What about?"

"Well, Eli was talking earlier about souls and what happens when you die. He seems to think that we have a soul and that it goes somewhere when we die."

"Yes."

"Well, do you agree with him?"

"Yes, I do," Seth answered with confidence. Benjamin was quiet. He was not sure what to say now. Benjamin looked down and twisted his fingers through the grass as he took hold of some and pulled it out.

"You disagree?" asked Seth.

Benjamin looked up. "Well, yes. You see, well, I don't believe in anything after death, or a soul for that matter," said Benjamin.

Seth looked hard at him and asked "Believe, or been taught to believe?"

Benjamin looked back down at the ground. "Well how could there be a soul?" he muttered.

Seth answered right back, "Why do you say that?" Benjamin was not sure how to answer. Seth added, "And why should there not be?"

Benjamin thought for a minute, "Well," he answered, "we get all our rewards for everything in this life. Not in some afterlife."

Seth half chuckled. "That always sounded to me like a good reason to live it up now and in whatever way you wanted. Have you not noticed it is more the rich and well off who think this? They do not want to be held responsible for how they live. What about those of us who are poor and have never had a way of getting richer? Did we do something wrong?" Seth asked. Then looking right at Benjamin he added in a soft voice, "What about those who did not do wrong themselves but suffer for other's wrongs."

Benjamin swallowed hard. He knew what Seth was talking about. He was talking about him suffering for his father. Taking a big breath and swallowing hard, Benjamin tried to get rid of the lump in his throat. "The sins of the father can be passed on to the children." He whispered in response. "It says so in Exodus 34:7, 'yet He will by no means leave the guilty unpunished, visiting the iniquity of fathers on the children and on the grandchildren to the third and fourth generations.'"

"Ah," replied Seth. "But it also says in Deuteronomy 24:16 'Fathers shall not be put to death for their sons, nor shall sons be put to death for their fathers; everyone shall be put to death for his own sin.'"

Benjamin thought for a minute. "Well, I am not dying for my father," he responded.

"No, I suppose not. And sometimes we do suffer for what our fathers have done. But all this does not show that there is no afterlife. I would think the argument could be made that because we are being punished for sins not our own that when we die things will be better in the hereafter," replied Seth.

Benjamin was quiet. He was not sure what to say, or think for that matter. He had only been taught one way and that was that there was no soul. This life was all we have and would ever have. But what if he was wrong? His father had told him so many lies. But others had told and taught him this way too. What if they were wrong too! How did one make sure they went to the good place and not the bad? Suddenly Benjamin spoke up, "Seth, do you think there is a place for good people and a place for bad people."

"Well, sure I do. The bad go to Hell or as the Greeks say, Hades. And the good to Heaven or Paradise," answered Seth.

"Well, how do you make sure you go to the good place and not to the bad place?"

"Well, you have to live right, you know, obey the law and all that. At least that is what I think." Seth smiled. "The Messiah will make it all clear when he comes. I just hope I live long enough to see and hear him for myself."

"You believe there will be a Messiah?"

"Well of course, don't you?"

"I guess so. That was something we did not talk a whole lot about in my synagogue," answered Benjamin.

"Oh, I look forward to the Messiah. It is said He will set all things right. He will be of the house and line of David. He will sit on David's throne. And if you ask me that would be a lot better than that Herod we have now."

Benjamin nodded. It did not seem like it would take much to be better than Herod. Although Herod was a great builder, he was even rebuilding the temple. But, the man was also crazy. He would kill his own wives and sons.

Seth looked over at Benjamin and said, "I know you do not find being a shepherd that great, but there were many great men in our history that were shepherds. King David was one. He would have taken care of his father's sheep in these very hills. God led him from here into greatness."

Benjamin hung his head. He knew Seth was trying to cheer him, but he was not feeling it tonight. "Well, David went from this to greater. Not from greater to this, like me," Benjamin answered back.

"Yes, but there were great men who were shepherds all their lives. Abraham, Isaac, Jacob, most of Jacob's sons, and even Moses was a shepherd for forty years. He went from the palaces of Egypt to being a shepherd, to leading the people out of slavery. See Benjamin, sometimes we have to be somewhere that we don't want to be, somewhere not that great, for a time."

"Yes, but what if I am here forever?" Benjamin answered back. "What then?"

Seth grinned, "Then we have to wait for the hereafter."

In spite of himself Benjamin had to smile back. They did not talk much after that and before long it was time to change the watch; then they were allowed to go back to sleep.

Benjamin woke to a cloudy sky that threatened rain. The sheep were restless too. All day they did not behave. They would either bunch up all together and refuse to move, or they would run in all directions. Benjamin got a lot of practice using his sling. He would sling stones in the direction of a wayward sheep to chase it back to the rest, or in the right direction. He was getting it more and more and all the earlier practices were helping. However, whether he helped or not, Benjamin was never quite sure. Sometimes the stones he slung seemed to work, and other times they seemed to make things worse. It did rain on them on and off. Once more Benjamin was thankful for his sheepskin mantel. He sure did not look his best, but he had to admit that it was the right kind of clothing to wear, even if he did not look very good. When night fell no one much felt like talking. All settled down early, and when it was Seth and Benjamin's time to watch, they did not do much talking. They both just concentrated on staying awake and staying warm.

The dreary weather lasted for a few days before it got nicer. It had served well to help Benjamin get hardened to the life of a shepherd. As more days slipped by, he got more used to the land and how one lived on and from it. He and Ethan did not talk much, but they tolerated each other and Benjamin did not feel quite so disliked by him.

When they would make camp at night, Benjamin felt more and more a part of the group. Most nights he would stay and listen to the talk, but he rarely said anything himself. He did not feel quite at that point. He would talk during the watch about random things with Seth. He liked Seth more and more and felt fully accepted by him.

Days would pass much the same way without much excitement. They would change pastures every now and again. One night they were wakened late in the night by shouts and yells. It would seem a bear had tried to sneak in to snatch a sheep but was heard by Caleb who was on watch. The bear was chased away by Caleb and the others as they woke up and helped. Benjamin only got a glimpse of a dark blob moving away. Part of him wished he could have been involved more, and part of him was glad he had not been closer.

As the days trickled by and as Benjamin became more accustomed to his work and lifestyle, he also found lots of time to think throughout the day. His thoughts often drifted to his father during these times. He thought over the last few years. His father had always been a busy man, but the last few years he had been even more so. He never seemed happy or even satisfied with anything. Nothing was ever good enough. The big thing that Benjamin remembered was that his father never liked being crossed. His father was right in everything. You never questioned that. His father always knew best. He always knew more then you. Benjamin had never been allowed to question anything his father said or did.

But now! Oh, but now Benjamin was questioning everything. Everything his father had done, said, and even what he had taught Benjamin. Of course Benjamin was taught not to steal, that was right in the ten big commands. But Benjamin's father had stolen. Were there other things that his father had gone back on? What if the things he had been taught were wrong too? These were the kind of thoughts that haunted Benjamin's mind.

One night on watch duty Benjamin was thinking about the things he had been taught. Without giving much thought to it, Benjamin turned to Seth and blurted out, "Do you believe in spiritual beings?"

"Like angels and such?" Seth asked.

"Yea," Benjamin replied.

"Sure I do. They are God's messengers and a lot more, I expect," Seth said looking over at Benjamin. "My guess is you don't believe in them."

"I have always been taught they are not real," Benjamin replied.

"What about all the angels throughout history?" asked Seth.

"Well," replied Benjamin, "only the Torah can really be trusted. It must have been something else, or people claiming to be seeing things."

"What about the Angel of Death during the first Passover?"

"It must have been a disease or something." Benjamin said in defense, but it sounded weak even to him.

"Sounds more like people believing what they want to believe," replied Seth looking at Benjamin. "Do you really believe all this, or is it just what you have been taught to say and think?" Benjamin looked down, not able to meet Seth's eyes. He knew that Seth knew the truth. "Don't you think it is time you started thinking for yourself and not just taking and believing everything you are told without examining it first?"

"But how do I know what or who to believe? I was taught everything one way, now I am hearing that it is all wrong. Who or what is right, and which is wrong?" Benjamin pleaded, he was feeling overwhelmed and confused.

"Oh, Benjamin. You have to figure that out for yourself. You have likely gotten most of Scripture memorized. You no doubt know it way better than I do. You have to remember it and think over it for yourself. You decide what you believe, not me, not your old teachers, not…most anyone else." Benjamin wondered if Seth was going to say his father. He would have been right. His father had told him what to believe. But now! Now he was being told to think for himself. It would be easiest to say he believed what he had always been told to believe, but truth be told, he was now questioning that, and he was not sure they were right.

"I will have to think on all this," Benjamin finally said.

"Good, you should think on it," Seth said. "Think on it good and hard. Don't jump to conclusions."

This is what Benjamin thought a lot of that night. The next night, however, something new was brought to their attention. They were all sitting down to eat when Amin told them the news. "People are soon going to be crawling all over here," he said.

"Why do you say that?" asked Caleb.

"Well not so much here as on the roads and in the towns and all." Amin replied. "You see, apparently the Emperor in Rome wants to take a census of everyone here. So everyone has to go to their own home to register."

Benjamin had been listening all along, but he looked up now. Did that mean he needed to go or do something? Did they all, and if they did who would take care of the sheep? When he was alone with Seth later, he asked him about this.

"You don't need to worry, son," he said. "Your uncle will take care of everything for you and likely me too. We are in his employment and have next to nothing of our own. We will be listed down under him and his care. Those with sheep of their own may have to register, but I doubt that will take too long."

Benjamin was relieved. Most would not be at all happy about this though. It would be inconvenient and bothersome, not to mention a reminder that Judah was not a free nation anymore but under the control of the pagan Romans. It would be interesting to have more people traveling around. But then again Benjamin realized he would likely see little of it, other than from a distance.

"We may need to watch the sheep more carefully when the time gets closer. We may or may not have much interaction with the travelers, but with this much going on there is no telling what sort of characters will be running around," Seth said.

It took a week for people to really start moving through. When the flock was kept close to the road or on a hill where the road could be seen, travelers could be seen passing along. Sometimes they traveled in large groups. Other times they traveled in ones or twos. Some brought their families while other men traveled alone.

This gave something for Benjamin to think on, but for the most part he thought about what he really believed. He would bring to mind and question so many things. He would then try to compare it with the Scriptures. Seth was right when he had said he likely knew the Scriptures. He had a lot of them memorized. He just had to think through them and find if they fit what he had been taught or if they said something different. It was also difficult to know just what some Scriptures meant when they said certain things. Much of it came back to one thing he had been taught that he was really beginning to think about. If he had been taught wrong it was going to mess with his mind.

One night Benjamin decided to talk to Seth about it. "Seth, I know you said I should try to figure things out for myself and decide what I

A Shepherd Tale

believe, but there is one thing I what to talk to you about," said Benjamin.

"Go ahead," replied Seth.

"Well there seems to be some Scripture that points to the idea of an afterlife and even the idea of angels. But all of this seems to point to one thing," stated Benjamin.

"And what is that?"

"That God still cares about His people, individually. I was always taught that God made the world, but He stopped caring about us individually, His people. I guess He must care a little or did when He gave Moses the Law and all. What do you think Seth?"

"I don't know, Benjamin. But I have always thought that God must care at least a little. He gets mad when we do things wrong or turn our back on Him. Just look at the Babylonian captivity. We also have the promise of the Messiah. Have you ever thought of that?"

"Do you really think there will be a Messiah? I know what He is suppose to be like. The Great Deliver who comes in and frees Israel from its enemies and rules over us Himself. I guess I am just not too sure about Him."

"Well I certainly hope there will be a Messiah, Benjamin. And as for God caring, I can tell you what I think. I think He does care. I think He knows about each one of us. But you have to decide all of this stuff for yourself, Benjamin. I also don't see how God could not be involved with us anymore when He has been so much throughout history. When the nation of Israel was under the control of Ahab, the prophet Elijah had a time where he wanted to give up. God told him He still had 7,000 people who had not bowed down to Baal or who had not kissed him. It says so in 1 Kings 19:18. I know it is a number but God knew and cared about each one of them. Yes, it may not seem like God has cared in a long time. But just because you can't see something does not mean it is not there."

"God still cares about you, Benjamin. I know things have been hard for you, and you think that if there is anything that could prove God can't see you or care about you, that it would be what has happened to you and where you are now. But that is not true. I can't prove it to you or show you in any way. I know we are the bottom of society and are the unseen and unwanted, but I am sure that God knows about us and cares. This is not your punishment for what your father did. You are not him. But also you need to let him go. You can't idolize him anymore, but neither should you hate him."

Benjamin thought for a moment. "I guess you are right about my father. I know now he was not the great, perfect man I always thought he was. I don't know that I hate him either. I will have to think about the whole God caring thing."

"You think about it, Benjamin," Seth said. "King David said in Psalm 139 that God made him and knew all about him before he was even born. Yes, he was a great man, but he was once a shepherd too. We never know what may happen to us and how great we may be." Benjamin nodded. He would think on it, but he doubted he would ever be great or that anything great would ever happen to him.

A few days passed and Benjamin thought a lot about God and whether He might really care about him or not. If God did know about him, would He punish Benjamin for his father's sins or would He not carry on the iniquities of the father to the son? And how did he, Benjamin, feel about his father?

One morning, a servant of his Uncle Asher's found them and said that Asher needed to talk to Seth. Seth said he likely wanted information on the flocks and how things were going. He assured Benjamin and Ethan that he should be back by night fall. Benjamin did not much like the idea of spending the day with Ethan, but he did not say anything and just waved goodbye to Seth as he walked away. The servant went with him, apparently figuring with two of them still here, he was not needed.

Benjamin and Ethan still did not talk much to each other, but Benjamin did not hate him either. They tolerated and worked around each other. In the afternoon when they were sitting on a hillside looking over the sheep below, Benjamin blurted out, "Do you dislike me, Ethan?" He froze. Why in the world had he said that? He had been thinking it, but he had not meant to say it aloud!

Ethan opened his eyes and sighed as he stared down over the sheep. "No," he replied. "I feel more sorry for you." Benjamin was surprised. "We have a lot in common though," Ethan continued. "I may have found it ironic at first that you ended up out here with me." Benjamin was confused at all this. Ethan looked over at him. "You don't even know what I am talking about, do you?" he said.

Benjamin shook his head no.

"Well did you know we are cousins?" he said.

"I thought we were related somehow," Benjamin replied.

Ethan nodded. "My mother and your father were brother and sister, along with Uncle Asher." He explained. "About eight or nine years ago, both of my parents died. My father did not have much family and the few that he did have were too poor to take me in. They would have liked to but could not. I was sent to your father, since he was the oldest of my mother's family. But, he claimed he could not take me, even though he had much more then my father's family. Neither he or nor Uncle Asher wanted to take me in. I believe it was your father who suggested I should be a shepherd for our Uncle Asher since he needed another one. I knew it was their way of getting rid of me since they did not have a reason for not taking me in, other than they did not want to. But I was younger than you and not used to high living like you. Also my family did not have the shame you have. They just died, where you carry the weight of your father's sin."

Benjamin was surprised. He thought they were related, but he had been too young to remember much. Now it made sense why Ethan had not liked him, or at least his family. They had turned him away for no reason. He would have been bitter too.

"I am sorry I haven't been nicer and more friendly to you, Benjamin," said Ethan.

"I haven't been overly friendly either," answered Benjamin. Ethan gave him a smile at this, and Benjamin smiled back. The rest of the day went well, and Benjamin found himself and Ethan talking a lot more to each other as they headed the sheep back to the resting place for the night.

They were now closer to Bethlehem and lights could be seen in the early part of the night. As the night would go on, the lights would go out. There were more lights than normal now because of all the people traveling. Nearly all would have found a place to stay, but the late comers would have been hard pressed to find any house with open space. There were a few lights from fires of people camping out.

Benjamin and Ethan drove the sheep in with the rest that had already been brought in. As the last of the other shepherds brought in their sheep, a lone figure was seen walking toward them. It was Seth. He was welcomed back by all, and they all sat down.

Seth then turned to Benjamin as he sat down by him and said, "Your mother was the first to greet me as I came to the house. She pounded me with questions, wanting to know how you were doing." Benjamin half expected the men to poke fun at him for this, but he was greeted rather with warm smiles from all. Seth continued, "Don't worry, Benjamin. I gave her a good report and told her that you missed her too." Seth said this as he gave him a pat on the back. "She also sent this for you," Seth added as he handed a sack to Benjamin. Surprised, Benjamin took it and slowly opened it. It was filled with bread, dried meat, and other food.

Caleb, who was sitting on the other side of him, looked down into the sack over his shoulder and gave a little whistle. "You will be eating well off that for days, Benjamin," he said. Benjamin continued looking into the sack. Caleb was right. He could eat well off this for days. He did not have to eat what was found out here. But, he would be eating it in front of the others. He had done just that when he first came with the food his mother had sent. But now he would feel odd and a little guilty if he ate all this in front of them.

"No, Caleb," he said as he looked up and around at all the faces he had come to know. "We will all eat well tonight."

"You don't have to do that, Benjamin. Your mother sent that for you," said Amin.

"I want to," replied Benjamin, and he found he really did want to share it. Benjamin then began to set it all out on the grass in front of them. Everyone was happy, and thanked him as they reached out to take something or tear it apart to share with the others. Seth then turned and handed something else to Benjamin. Benjamin took it with surprise. He was not expecting anything else. He was even more surprised when he examined it and found it to be a new sling. He looked up at Seth questioningly.

Seth smiled and said, "In your mother's inquiry I told her you were pretty good with a sling. She was all worried then because that was something she had not sent with you. I assured her and told her that I had given you an old extra I had. Well before I left, she handed me this for you. She went and bought it new in the market." Benjamin fingered his new sling. He had not expected this. He pulled out Seth's borrowed one and handed it back to him. Seth laughed and took it back. Still holding the new sling, Benjamin thought about what Seth had said.

"I am not very good with the sling though, Seth," he said.

"Sure you are," put in Ethan. "I think it must have taken me two years to get as good as you are now. And even now I am not very good with a sling." Benjamin was surprised by the praise but thanked him for it.

Everyone was in good spirits tonight. In their talking they would include Benjamin by asking his point on what they were talking about or what he thought about it. Ethan was often the one to do this as well. Seth observed this and smiled. He knew something must have happened while he was gone.

The next day was a good one, but nothing much out of the ordinary. Benjamin tried out his new sling and liked it very much. When evening fell they all gathered again. As Benjamin sat around with the others he realized that he would never have imagined his life like this, or that he would not mind it. He realized how like his father he had been, proud and arrogant. He had looked down on these very kinds of people. He had now become a new person, a better person. He had been like his father, too, in that he had not really been happy. To his surprise he was full of more joy now! He was thankful and found joy in the small things. He was more content. He would have never thought it was possible to be happy living like this. There were, of course, still questions and things he did not understand. What was God really like?

He had thought he know everything spiritual well enough. Now he was beginning to think he did not know much at all.

When it came time for Seth and Benjamin's watch, they sat on the grassy ground with their backs to the circle of sheep and stared out at the darkness beyond. They would regularly twist themselves around to scan and keep watch in all directions. The watch started out normal enough. Benjamin and Seth talked about random things and Seth would tell him stories of things that had happened in his younger days of shepherding.

Suddenly, and seemingly out of nowhere, a figure was standing over them. Benjamin let out a yell of surprise, and even though he was sitting down he nearly fell over. Seth turned deathly white and could be seen trembling beside him.

The surprise was due in part by the figure's sudden appearance. He was not there one second, and the next he appeared out of nowhere. But it was the figure's appearance. He stood over them and Benjamin was not sure if he just seemed really tall because they were sitting down, or if he was really that tall. The other big thing was the light. Light seemed to come from him and from all around him. His clothes were brilliant, and light even seemed to come from the sword at his side. Benjamin stared at the figure wondering who he was and where he came from, when the truth dawned on him. He sucked in his breath hard. This was not a man! This was an ANGEL! They were real! Here was one right in front of him.

A new wave of fear rushed over Benjamin. He had doubted angels even existed. He glanced at the angel's huge sword. What if this angel knew about that? Would he cut Benjamin down? The sword made it perfectly clear this angel was not to be messed with. All the other stories of angels came back to Benjamin's mind. There were plenty of stories of them being sent to kill people. Benjamin stole a look behind him. The light from the angel lit up half the hillside. Benjamin could see the other shepherds were all awake and staring as well. Benjamin turned back to the angel. Seth was still rooted in the same place. The light and sheer presence of the angel could only be described in one word, Glory, really the Glory of the Lord.

The angel then began to speak. He told them to have no fear for behold he had come to preach and proclaim a divine message of momentous joy and gladness which was for all people. This was because delivered and born to them this very day in the city of David, Bethlehem, was a Savior, a deliverer, who was the Messiah, the Lord. And a sign for them would be that they would find a newborn baby wrapped in cloth and lying in a manger.

The angel had barely stopped speaking when another wonder of wonders happened. All around the first angel was a great throng of a heavenly army of angels. They were telling and celebrating and praising God. They were giving glory to and praising God from the highest heavens, as God was the Highest of the High, and saying that on the earth below, peace, and rest with man whom God was well pleased.

When the angels were done praising God they left again, back to heaven it would seem. At first, Benjamin was too stunned and surprised to move. Had that just happened? He turned to look at Seth. Seth was still rooted in the same spot staring at where all the angels had been. Slowly the other shepherds gathered around them.

"Where did the first one come from?" asked Ethan.

"I don't know," answered Benjamin. "He was just there all of a sudden, out of nowhere really."

"Where did they go?" asked Jeb.

"Back to heaven I would say," put in Amin.

"I can't believe I just saw angels," said Jethro.

"What does it all mean?" asked Jubal.

"It means we should go to Bethlehem," stated Eli.

"Agreed," said Seth suddenly, finally moving from his fixed position to stand. "Come; let us all go to Bethlehem to see this wonderful thing that God has told us about."

Everyone began to agree. Benjamin got to his feet, and they all started to walk in the direction of Bethlehem. He still felt like he was in shock.

Suddenly Jeb stopped and asked, "What about the sheep? We should not just leave them."

"I think they will be fine," put in Caleb. "If God decided to tell us this news, I think He will watch over them for us tonight." The others seemed to agree. At any rate no one wanted to stay behind.

As they walked, Benjamin hurried up beside Seth, "What does all this mean?" he asked.

Seth looked down at him in surprise. "Didn't you hear what the angel said?" he asked. "It means that this very day, in Bethlehem, the Messiah has been born. And, we, of all people, get to see Him. It would seem that heaven was too full of joy to contain itself."

"But why tell us?"

"I don't know." Seth answered. Then smiling, he put an arm around Benjamin's shoulders and added, "Maybe God does care about us lowly shepherds after all."

Benjamin was surprised. Could this mean that God did care about them, the lowest of the low? Could this mean that God cared about him? He had not been sure God even know he existed, and he figured if God did know about him it was only to pass judgment and punishment onto him from his father. But it was true; God had sent angels to him along with the others.

Benjamin started thinking over all the angels had said. They said that the Messiah had been born. Benjamin had always heard that the Messiah would be a great man. But even great men had to be born. But if he was a great man, would he not be born to a great family? The angel said he would be in a manger. Mangers were normally in stables. What was a great family doing in a stable? There was something else that seemed a little strange, too. "Seth," he asked, "what did the angel mean when he said Messiah the Lord? Did he mean that he would be a Master and a Lord or did he mean Lord God?"

"I don't know, Benjamin?" said Seth. "It did seem a bit strange, didn't it?"

Benjamin nodded but there was too much to think about to dwell on this too long.

They had walked fast and made it to Bethlehem rather quick. They then began to check the stables, after all, the angel had said the baby would be in a manger, and mangers were most times in with the animals in the stables.

They first checked some stables that were on the outskirts of Bethlehem, but they found nothing.

"What do we do now? Should we waking people and asking if they have a newborn baby in their stable?" asked Jeb with a hint of sarcasm in his voice.

"Maybe we should," answered Jubal.

"First let's go to Samuel's place. He is likely to have a lot of people staying with him," put in Amin. Benjamin was not sure who this Samuel was, but they all started to wind their way through the city. As they went, they checked all the stables that were open or easy to get to. They listened for a baby's cry or any sign of people being in the stable. With so many people traveling through, it may not be all that out of the ordinary for people to be staying in a stable. Most stables were just a room on the side of the house.

As they hurried through the city they came to a larger house. This house went more up than out as some did. The first floor seemed to dip down into the ground. The door was open and a little light could be seen coming out. They walked up to the door and looked down in. It was a stable, and what was more, they could see a man and a woman. The couple was off to one side on a elevated place made for a servant to sleep on and attend to things in the stable. They walked into the stable and toward the couple. Benjamin also noted a boy his own age standing off to one side, but he was focused on the small wooden box set between the two people. They had been in a great hurry to get here, but now they slowed and peered into the manger. There, to their great joy, was a tiny baby all wrapped up.

Seth was the first to speak. "The Lord God has spoken truth to us this night. All that the angel said is true," he said in a shocking voice.

"An angel?" asked the young man. He seemed interested but not nearly as surprised as Benjamin thought he would be. The other shepherds began to explain what had happened, and what had been said to them. As they did this Benjamin was observant. The man and woman both looked tired, especially the woman. They also looked young, younger than what he would have expected. Benjamin slipped up and peered down at the baby then drew back again. He was so tiny! The angel had said a newborn, but Benjamin had not thought about that much, and he had never been around many newborns. The angel had said a Savior was born, but this baby was helpless. He could do nothing for himself, but He was the Messiah. The Messiah!

Benjamin stepped up again to look at the baby. Staring at it, something struck him. Just looking at this baby, no one would guess that this baby was the Messiah. He was little and helpless, how could he be the deliverer of Israel? Benjamin looked at the baby's parents; they were young and obviously poor. His own people would not think much of them. It hit Benjamin then that God did not care what people looked like, who their parents were, or even where they came from. It was not that God did not know, but that He did not care and would use them anyway. This could be true for him too. God knew who he was, who his parents were, and where he was. Even with all this, God had let him see the angels and hear their message. And what was more, He had let Benjamin see the Messiah.

The man and women had a few questions about all that had happened. They were amazed, but they also seemed to share some secret glances when they talked about the angels. The shepherds learned that the man's name was Joseph and the lady was Mary. The little tiny baby Messiah was named Jesus. They were told that they could touch him if they were gentle and were careful not to wake him. They were all a little slow, but one by one they did. Benjamin even took his turn. The baby was so little; Benjamin just could not get over it. Reluctantly, they realized they should be leaving. They needed to get back to their sheep and the young couple needed to get some sleep. Dawn would come before they knew it.

As they left, they could not stop talking about all they had seen and what had happened. They were continually giving praise to God. They did not care so much anymore if they woke people. Benjamin joined in the praising and felt no shame. He did not care if people heard him and were mad. He was too full of joy. He was also not ashamed of being seen with the group. This was who he was now and these men were truer friends of his than what he had ever had.

As they left the city and stared out over the fields, they grew quieter, each lost in his own thoughts. Benjamin was thinking about how he had had so many questions about God. He had been taught that God was not involved in our personal lives, but it would seem He was. God knew Joseph and Mary and was very much involved in their lives even though they were poor. He knew all about, and was already involved in, the life of baby Jesus, and even Benjamin himself. He had wondered so much, even about angels, and now he knew. God was real and involved in the lives of His people. He had sent them a Messiah just as He promised. He cared about them, even a shepherd boy.

"Seth," he said turning to him as they reached the sheep. "Will anyone believe us about this after tonight?"

Seth laughed and most of the other shepherds joined in with him. "No, son, likely not. They will say it's just a wild shepherd's tale. They don't believe much of anything we say anyway," he replied. "But don't worry. We know it happened, and that what we say is true. As for me, I know I have experienced the best thing in my life tonight, and I will never forget it. And I will also be content for the rest of my days, knowing God spoke to me, and I saw his words fulfilled."

Benjamin pondered about what he had said as dawn came. They separated their sheep and all headed out across the fields. They were reluctant to leave each other after such a night. Benjamin knew they would all be exhausted come night again. As his group started out over a hill, Benjamin stopped and looked back at all the other groups heading out. This experience had brought them all closer together as a group. He knew again that he was one of them and was glad for it. Also he was no longer troubled about God. He knew lots, but there were still lots of things he did not understand. But even that was okay. God knew of him and cared about him just as he was. Benjamin smiled as he hurried to join up with Seth and Ethan. God had given him peace, a place to belong, and Benjamin knew he was loved. He was loved by God.

At the End of the Journey

Javed took one more look at the sky and then wrote down a few more things. The sun would soon start to show its rays on the eastern horizon, and then it would come up in all its golden glory. Javed gathered his things and started down the hill. One of the great rivers was off to the right and the other was a little way to the left of him. He needed to get back; for once Omid was awake, he would want a report.

And what would Javed tell him? Javed would tell him that the night sky was much like it always was. The stars were in their places, and so all was right and good in the world. All that is, but that one star. It had not done much this night, but it had done enough in the past few nights to make all the star watchers focus most intently on it.

These star watchers were the Magi, or sometimes called wise men, studiers of nature and how things worked. They were counselors and close officials of the kings of the Parthian Empire and were respected around the world. Like all Magi, they mostly studied the stars, but these Magi of the East studied many things.

Javed was the personal slave of Omid, the oldest and wisest of this order of Magi. There were hundreds of Magi, but two of the most important ones of this time were Arman and Kian. Arman's main focus was on the stars. Kian studied more of the natural laws of the world. They often worked hand-in-hand with things. But if they ever had questions or something puzzled them, they always went to Omid. Omid had done it all. The king of the Parthian Empire had said he was the smartest man in the world. But Omid was a humble man and never claimed this. He was content to study and learn all he could. Even now, when his eyes had failed him, he did not stop. Javed was his eyes. Some nights, like this past one, Omid would send him out to study the stars and report on their locations. He liked to keep up on it all. Omid knew Javed would tell him exactly as it was and would not leave out a thing. But most days Omid would have Javed read to him. This was the studying that Omid was doing now.

Javed had been a slave all his thirteen years to Omid, as had Javed's father before him. Javed knew he was privileged more than most free men ever would be. He had grown up learning at his father's side all the ways of the Magi. Not only could he read and write many languages, but he knew the stars and many of the natural laws. Javed had studied at his father's side until his father had died two years ago. Then Omid began to teach Javed even more. Omid was the best master a man could ask for, but Javed still had a longing to be free. Not that he would ever tell anyone. He was very grateful for all he had, and he knew most would not understand his wish to be free. So it was best to never think, much less talk, about freedom.

Javed continued on the path that led down the hill and on around until it came to the small town where the Magi lived. The Magi lived all over but this was one of their favorite places. The sun was just starting to rise when Javed reached the house of Omid. He hurried through the house to Omid's sleeping chamber. Stopping outside the doorway, Javed peeked his head past the curtained doorway. Inside two other slaves were helping Omid dress. One of them noted Javed and turned to Omid and whispered in his ear.

"Come in, Javed," Omid called out. "I thought I heard you come in."

Javed slipped into the room and bowed before his master. Even though Omid could not see him perform this action, Javed would never have dreamed of not bowing to his master upon entering.

"Master," he said.

"Ah, you have been out watching the stars for me, have you not, my son?" Omid said.

"Yes, my Lord," answered Javed.

"And you have your notes for me?"

"Yes, my Lord."

"Good! Have you eaten yet?"

"No, my Lord."

"Ah, then you will eat with me this morning."

After stating this Omid held out his hand. Javed understood he was to take Omid's hand and lead him to the room were the slaves always set up his meals. Javed often ate with Omid, but it was by no means a common action. Most of the other free men would never dream of eating with a slave. When Javed ate with Omid, he would help Omid get whatever he wanted as well as eat himself. Javed knew today to he would read his notes from his night of watching the stars.

Javed guided Omid into the dining room and seated him on his cushions at the head of the table. He then seated himself down from Omid but close enough that he could assist Omid when needed. As they ate Javed told Omid all he had seen and written down.

"And anything new from our special star?" asked Omid.

"Not this night, my Lord," answered Javed.

"Hmm," was all that Omid said. After eating, Javed guided Omid into his study.

"What do you want me to read to you today, my Lord?" he asked.

"Let us continue were we left off," answered Omid, "in the Hebrew book written by their prophet Isaiah."

Javed was not surprised by this choice. He had figured they would continue were they had left off. Omid had had him reading from many Hebrew texts lately.

Years before, the nation of Judea had been conquered by the Babylonian Empire. Many of the Jewish people had been taken as prisoners to Babylon. They had remained in Babylon for some seventy years until the Meds and Persians had taken over the Babylonian Empire. King Cyrus had allowed the Jews to return to their homeland. Some returned and made the nation of Judea. That land was now a part of the Roman Empire.

But not all the Jews went back. Some remained in their captive homeland. During their captivity by the Babylonians, there were even a few who became wise man or Magi. The greatest of these was a man named Daniel. The Babylonians had called him Belteshazzar. He had brought in many of his Jewish beliefs and holy books to the Magi's keeping of that time. Now a few hundred years later, some things were different, but much remained. This region that they were in was not far from the former city of Babylon. Javed also knew that Omid had some Jewish heritage.

Javed picked up the scroll off the table, after he had gotten Omid seated, and then he then seated himself. Javed did not care for this book much. Some of the Jewish books were very interesting but this one talked about destruction of certain nations. It also had a lot of prophecies concerning the destruction and return of Israel. Javed was not sure if these things had already happened because this book was written before the Babylonian captivity, or if this referred to something else, something yet to come. There were some things that were really interesting in this book though. As he started reading, he soon found himself reading aloud about someone who would suffer greatly.

As he finished this passage and continued on to the next, Omid stopped him. "Reread that for me," he said.

"Which part?" asked Javed, "from where I started?"

"From where it first started talking about the man who will suffer."

Javed found the place and began to read again. This was common. Omid wanted to hear things again so he could better understand them. When Javed reached the end, Omid told him to stop. Javed knew he was thinking over what was read. If he wanted to, he might share with Javed what he was thinking.

After a long pause Omid spoke. "Have you ever heard this passage before?"

"No, my Lord," Javed answered.

Omid went on to explain the passage, although Javed had for the most part understood it from reading it. "This passage speaks of a great man who will suffer. But even though he suffers he will not cry out or protest. He knows what he is doing and why. Javed, I believe this man is the same man that the Jews refer to as the Messiah, a great man who is sent to deliver them. They believe he will be a great king and will deliver them from the Romans who now control them. But this passage makes me wonder. Maybe he will not deliver them in the way they think."

"You do not think he will be their Great Deliverer?"

"Oh, yes I do. He will be the greatest of all men, but I wonder if he will deliver as they believe he will deliver."

Javed did not know what Omid meant by this, but he tucked this conversation back in his mind to remember later.

Javed continued to read to Omid, but it was not long before he began to feel very tired. He had been up all night, watching the stars and had not had much extra sleep the day before. He did not bring this up to Omid though. This was a part of being a slave; one did not complain, at least not to your master. Omid was a wise old man though. Finally he stopped Javed. "Stop, Javed. I have been trying to decide what is wrong with your voice; now I realize it is because you are tired. You have been up all night and now need to sleep."

"I am fine, my Lord," Javed protested.

"No, I insist. Go sleep. I shall be fine. I shall have one of the others read to me. No, they are not as good as you, but they will do fine as you rest."

Javed rose to his feet and bowed to his master. "Yes, my Lord." He left the room and soon found one of the other many household slaves and told him that his master wished to have someone else come and read to him. From there Javed went to his own small room and lay down. Before he fell asleep Javed thanked the gods, including the Jewish God if he could hear him, and his lucky stars that he had such a merciful master.

For the next several days Javed continued to read to Omid. The mysterious star kept up its work of moving around and doing things a star did not do. Before long there was talk of having a large meeting of the Magi to discuss the star and what it meant. Omid had Javed keep reading to him from Jewish books and not just one or straight through. He wanted to hear certain passages over and over. He also had other slaves write letters for him. Javed was not sure what all was going on in Omid's mind, but he knew not to ask. If he was to know, he would be told.

The day of the meeting arrived. It was to be held in Omid's house in one of his largest rooms. Omid instructed Javed to put a good number of certain scrolls in the room near where he was to be seated. Omid was to have the seat of honor because this was his house, and he was considered one of the oldest and wisest. As the hour for the meeting drew closer, more and more guests, primarily Magi, arrived. Javed was busy helping the other slaves when Omid sent for him.

"My Lord," he said entering the room and bowing to Omid.

"Javed, you shall stand by me in the meeting today. I will need you to be my eyes and read what I instruct you to read."

Javed bowed again feeling a tingle of excitement go through him. "It will be a great honor my Lord," he said. He had hoped he would be chosen for this task. He had been in many meetings before but never one this big and important.

Omid held out his hand. "Help me into the meeting, my boy," Omid said with a smile. Javed took Omid's hand and helped him to stand, then guided him to the meeting room where he guided him to his cushioned seat. Then Javed took his place standing behind Omid.

Some of the Magi whispered among themselves as the last of the guests arrived. Finally it was announced that all were present. Arman then stood and began talking about the star. He explained in depth about what it did and did not do. He explained what it did that was not normal and why. Most of this was more or less known by all, but it was customary to lay it all out so nothing was omitted or confusing. Arman also had several other Magi come up and speak. These were man who were very high in their own right and had studied this star a great deal. After him, Kian got up and spoke. He did not have as much to say for he did not study the stars as much, but he explained how other things may be connected to this. After him, it was opened up to all to speak about what they thought of this star.

It was not long before it was agreed upon by all that this star proclaimed the birth of a great king or leader. It seemed unlikely that this was for their own Parthian Empire. It seemed to denote some other country. A Magi by the name of Malek stood and suggested that this was for the nation of Judah. He gave his reasons and references as to why he thought this.

After this Kian turned to Omid and asked, "O wise Omid, you have not graced us with your voice this whole counsel. We all know you are the wisest and most learned among us. What think you of all this? I know you have studied this star and what it may mean. I pray, tell us your thoughts." All the other Magi chimed in their wishes to hear his opinion.

Omid stared straight ahead. "Javed, please read from the scroll written by the Jewish prophet Isaiah. Read the part concerning the maid having a child," Omid commanded. Javed hurried to find the scroll and to then find the exact place. This was one of the passages that Omid had had Javed read to him several times. Javed found the place and proceeded to read how a young maiden or virgin girl would give birth to a child, and the child would be called Immanuel. (Isaiah 7:14) The room was silent for a minute before Kian spoke.

"This is a very interesting prophecy, especially considering under normal circumstances this would be impossible. But what does this have to do with the star?"

"You shall see in a moment when I explain," Omid said. Then after a pause he continued. "I agree with Malek that this star is to say that a great leader is to come to the nation of Judah. According to what the star has most recently done, I would say the child has been born. The star's first movements may have been in relation to this leader's conception and so the beginning of his life." Omid proceeded to explain all of the star's movements in light of this. By the time Omid was done giving his explanations, all were nodding in agreement.

Omid then began to speak again. "However, that is not all. This is where the prophecy that I had Javed read comes into play. This child, that it talks of, is who the Jews call the Messiah, Anointed One. They believe he will become their king and deliver them from their enemies. At this time, that would be the Roman Empire."

At this point Omid had Javed read several more passages that he had been studying of late. Javed was now putting it all together. All these Jewish prophecies that Omid had been studying were of this Messiah figure.

After Javed finished reading through several prophecies, Omid began to speak again. "I believe this man will be one of the greatest men the world has ever seen, and the world will never be the same because of him. This sort of birth is one that calls for a trip of homage to be made to see this new King of the Jews."

A clamor of agreement went up from the Magi in the room. It was then that Arman spoke up, "I agree that we should go see this new king, but we must discuss a few things. This baby is no doubt in Judah, and Judah is a part of the Roman Empire. Although the Parthian Empire and the Romans may be at peace for now, we should still tell our king of our plans."

"As to that," said Omid, "I have already taken care of it. I wrote a letter to the king letting him know there may be a party of Magi going into the Roman Empire to pay homage to a great child who has been born. He has written me to say he would send some soldiers with us for protection. However, I do not think that a wise idea. We all have bodyguards who are better than common soldiers. I think we should go with them. They will protect us better and are less likely to cause trouble than common soldiers."

Again the assembly agreed to Omid's suggestion. Someone asked how they were to find this king, to which it was answered that he would likely be in the Jewish holy city of Jerusalem, and if he was not there then the Jewish people should know where their king was.

Then the question was asked as to who was going on this journey. It was soon determined that Arman and Kian would go since they were the two top Magi under Omid. They were also the top in their two different areas. They both wished to have some other Magi from their same departments, Wiseman, who were up and coming with a wide knowledge of many things. Under Arman, with well-versed knowledge of the stars as well as other things, were chosen Mohsem and Hashem. Under Kian was chosen Utabar and Malek who understood many natural laws as well as had knowledge of other things that could be useful on the trip.

Mohsem was best in mathematics. Hashem was a wonderful astronomer, though most Magi were. Hashem was known for his knowledge in astronomy. Arman himself was big into astrology, although there too, many Magi were. Kian was the best in the natural sciences. Utabar was a doctor and well-versed in medicine. And Malek was the scholar.

All were excited, and for a time the room was a buzz of talk without any order. Then Arman turned from Kian to speak to Omid. Above the noise his voice spoke out, "O great Omid, we would be most honored if you would come with us on this great journey." The room quieted at this, and all heads turned once more to Omid.

"No, Arman, I cannot make this journey," said Omid.

"It would be no trouble," interrupted Arman. "We will go slower for you and make sure all is comfortable. Please Omid, we wish to have you on this trip."

Omid held up his hand. "You interrupted me, Arman," he said. "No, this is a journey I must forgo. But I have a different plan. I shall send another in my place. One who shall go in my name. He will write down all that takes place. He shall be my eyes and ears. He shall be all that I cannot be."

"As you wish, Omid. Whom do you have in mind? I know you well enough to know you already have someone in mind for this great honor," said Arman.

"You are right, Arman," said Omid. "I do have someone picked. I wish my personal slave Javed to go in my place."

Javed's eyes got big, and he froze to the spot where he stood. He had had no idea of this happening. All eyes in the room turned to him. Most were full of surprise, others had concern or contempt for him.

"Javed has been my slave all his life. His father was my most trusted slave, and Javed learned at his father's side. Now that his father is dead, Javed has taken his place. He will know just what to write and what to leave out. He knows better than anyone else what I will want," said Omid.

The room was silent for several very long seconds. Then one of the Magi asked, "My Lord Omid, may I speak freely?"

"Of course," replied Omid.

"My Lord, these great men will be going to a land that is not a part of the Parthian Empire. If this slave of yours should decide to run away, it will be very hard to get any help catching him. He is a mere slave, a boy. Would it not be better to send a true Magi in your place and not this slave?" "My friend," replied Omid. "There is no one better. I trust

Javed not to run away. Also you forget that there will be other slaves going on this journey. Javed will be expected to carry his weight of work as well as keep track of things for me. And if you are still worried that he will run, I have a very good reason for him to come back. When he returns from this journey for me, I intend to set him free. So you see, he would have no reason to run away in a foreign land where he may be taken as a slave by another. When, if he returns, he will receive his freedom."

Javed's head snapped down to look at Omid. Could he be series? Freedom!

No fuss was made about this by the other Magi. The talk continued on about the coming journey, but Javed could not keep his mind on the talk; it was too full of other things. Freedom! He was to have his freedom. How did Omid know he wanted his freedom? He might not know, but with Omid there was a good chance he did know. Also he was to make this trip. As soon as Omid had mentioned this trip, he had thought how wonderful it would be to go. To travel and see other lands and people would be wonderful. And then to see a baby king, who was destined to become a great man, would be wonderful too.

But he had known that Omid could not make this trip. He was too old and it would be too hard for him without his sight. Then Omid said he, Javed, was to go. That was the greatest honor he could ever receive from Omid, and he could barely believe it even now that he was to go on this journey. And not just as a slave but in Omid's name. Then Omid had said that if Javed would but do this for him and return, he would receive his freedom. Javed was having trouble take it all in.

Finally the meeting was brought to a close. The Magi who were to go on this journey were to remain in the room with Omid. All the others could leave. Slowly the rest left the room, still full of excitement for plans made and what had been brought forth.

After all the others had left, the remaining six Magi drew closer and sat down. Javed remained standing behind Omid.

Kian was the first to speak. "We need to figure out what route we are going to take," he said.

"We also should think about gifts," put in Hashem. "If we are going to pay homage to a king, we should not go empty-handed."

"I agree with you, Hashem," said Omid. "As to the traveling routes, I will leave that to you six. You should talk among yourselves as to what gifts you think best to take. I already have in mind what I shall send with Javed. Let us meet in two days to discuss more plans. I am weary now, and that should give you enough time to plan among yourselves. Remember when you plan gifts that you are going to Jews, and you will have a far distance to go too. And do not forget that you will be in the Roman Empire. I will not be traveling with you, but I may send a fair amount of things with Javed."

The others agreed that whatever he wished to send would be fine. After a little more talk, the six Magi rose to their feet and left the house.

"Ah, now that is over. Javed help me up; I am rather spent," commented Omid.

It was late in the evening now. The meeting with all the discussion had taken most of the afternoon. It was now time for the evening meal and some household slaves had already prepared and set it out.

Javed helped Omid recline on his cushions to eat. Javed remained standing behind Omid, lost in his own thoughts until Omid's voice called him back to the present. "Are you not going to sit and eat with me, Javed?" asked Omid.

Javed gave a start. "If...if you wish, my Lord," stammered Javed dragging his thoughts back to the present. Javed sat down and Omid continued to eat, however Javed barely did. His mind was still too full and could not quiet down yet.

When Omid was done eating, he asked, "Are you sure you don't want any more to eat, Javed?"

Once more Javed was jolted back to the present. "Thank you, my Lord," said Javed looking down at his hands. "But I think I have eaten all I can right now."

Omid nodded. "Then how about you take me to my study. We have things we need to talk about."

"Yes, my Lord," answered Javed, who hurried to his feet to help Omid up. Once they were in the study and Omid was settled, he motioned for Javed to sit down across from him. Omid waited until he heard Javed sit down, and then he began. "Now, Javed, how about you tell me what you are thinking," said Omid.

Javed was not excepting this. He thought they were discussing the trip and what was needed and what he would have to do. He fumbled a bit trying to put his jumbled thoughts into words.

"Well, my Lord, you see," Javed stopped. How to say what was in his head? "My Lord," he said starting over. "It is a great honor. I did not expect to be able to go on this trip. It is the greatest honor I could ever expect to receive. But the matter that is most on my mind," Javed paused. How did he go about this?

"The matter of receiving your freedom is what is most on your mind?" spoke Omid.

Javed's head snapped up in surprise. How had he known? "My Lord, I have never spoken about wanting my freedom."

"Never the less, you have wanted it."

"How did you know, my Lord?"

"Most slaves want their freedom. It is true that the older they get, the more they tend to accept their lot in life. Also most slaves would not know how to live free or have a means to do so. However you do. You are smarter and know more than most free men." Omid paused for a moment. "Your father always wanted his freedom and freedom for his family. You are your father's son, and you are much like him. I always thought that one day I would give him his freedom, but I waited too long. Your father was my best friend and also almost like a son to me. You are the grandson that I could never have. I waited too long to give your father his freedom, so I decided I would not make the same mistake with you. I wanted to wait until your were old enough to make it on your own, and to know enough. I merely needed a reason to set you free."

Javed was surprised beyond words. He felt hot tears form at the corners of his eyes. Omid thought of him as his grandson! To know that someone cared about him was a great feeling. In a way he had always known that Omid cared about him but this confirmed it. And in a way this was more. He thought of him like family, and that was special.

"Javed," said Omid bringing him back again. "There is something more I want you to do. This is not something I want you to do for me though. This is something I want you to do for yourself. I have had copies made of all the Hebrew Scriptures. I want you to take those copies with you and to read and study them as often as you can. Let me explain myself further. If this baby is the promised Savior, the Messiah, as the Jews call him, he is needed. He is needed for more than just the Jews. The whole world and all people need a Savior. The Jews believe that he will deliver them from their physical enemies, but from my studies, I think he will do more.

"You and I, and all people need to be forgiven for the bad things we do. All people make sacrifices to their gods to appease them or seek favor. The Jews do the same. But with all of the animals that are sacrificed, can they save us from the punishments we deserve? I believe this Messiah will do more than save the Jews from their physical enemies. The Scriptures speak different places about someone who will come and suffer greatly for the Jewish people, and to my understanding, do this for their sins. Sins are the bad and wrong things people do. I believe this Messiah is that person. He will save them, and maybe from their own sins if not from their enemies. Do you understand what I am saying, Javed?" asked Omid.

"I think so, my Lord."

"Good, this is why I want you to study the Jewish Scriptures for yourself as much as possible. It will also help you understand the people and culture you are going into."

Omid paused again in thought, and then he continued. "I am too old and too far away to fully convert to Judaism. I am who and what I am. But Javed you are young, and with your freedom you can go wherever you wish. If this Messiah is only for the Jewish people, you have a chance yet to convert to Judaism. If the God of Abraham, Isaac, and Jacob is merciful, perhaps he will accept me, for I have stopped all worship to other gods and only sacrifice to Him, but I don't know if this is enough. But Javed, you have a chance yet. I want you to think about this very seriously."

"But my Lord, I am not Jewish. I am an outsider to them, a Gentile. Would they ever accept me?"

"Others have been accepted. You may have to do some things and renounce old processes. It may not be easy, but I do think it is possible though." Javed was silent. This was a whole new idea to him. "This is entirely your decision, Javed. No one can make you do any of this," said Omid. "Think about it."

"Yes, my Lord," Javed answered nodding his head. He could not think to say any more at the moment.

"We shall talk more tomorrow about all of this. I think you should go to bed now. You have much to think on. Sleep some too, if you can," Omid added with a smile.

"Do you need me to lead you to your chamber first?" Javed remembered to ask.

"No. I have some thinking to do myself. I will call one of the other servants when I am ready."

Javed rose and bowed to Omid before leaving and going to his own mat for the night.

It was a long time before Javed could sleep. Too much had happened this day. First, finding out he was to go on a great journey bearing Omid's name would have been enough to keep him up late. Then to be told at the journey's end he was to receive his freedom was beyond his wildest dreams. Now Omid had added to the mix the idea of converting to Judaism. He was not sure how he felt about this. He did not think much of the common gods because Omid did not pay homage to them. He did not think the stars determined your life but rather foretold what it was to be like.

He had always taken whatever Omid said as word. Omid's word was good enough for him. In a way, it was the slave driven into him. He was not to think as much for himself but to take whatever Omid, his master, said as truth. But now he was to be a free man and Omid wanted him to study the Scriptures for himself and come up with his own conclusion. It was all new and confusing to him. There was too much to think on. He was to go and see more of the world. And after that he was to be free. What would he do then? Would he convert to

Judaism? Would they and their God accept him? Would he be worthy of this one God?

Late in the night Javed fell into a fitful sleep. When Javed awoke the next morning the house was abuzz with noise. The news of the trip was now known. Javed was soon put to work. He learned that Omid was not only sending him but was helping to finance the whole trip. Supplies and food had to be gotten together and prepared. Plenty of horses had to be gotten as well for transportation. The strong Persian stead was their normal means of transportation. This journey would be no different in that. Javed was thankful he could ride, even if he was not nearly as good as some.

As Javed was kept busy with his hands and feet, his mind was busy too, thinking over every detail of the day before. He went over every tiny detail. He had much to think about. What would happen at the journey's end? But that was still a long way off, and there were other things he need to focus on now. Finally he came to the conclusion that for now he needed to focus on the journey. Preparations needed to be made now. Also on their trip he would still be a slave and have work to do, not to mention that Omid wanted him to study the Hebrew Scriptures he was sending with Javed.

The day was spent in a hurried flurry, and Javed saw very little of Omid. Late in the evening though, Omid did summon him. When Javed arrived in Omid's personal chamber and gave his customary bow, he noticed someone else was also in the room. It was Zafar, one of Omid's personal bodyguards whenever he went places. Omid had no enemies that Javed knew of, but it was always good to be prepared especially considering Omid was very wealthy and one of the most sought after men in the Parthian Empire.

Zafar was a young man and very robust. He stood straight and tall in the corner, rippling muscles showing and armed to the teeth. He was a slave like Javed, but he was respected and revered.

"You summoned me, my Lord?" said Javed.

"Yes, Javed. On this trip you will still be a slave, but you are going in my name, and so I want you protected," said Omid. With a wave of his hand, Zafar stepped forward and Omid continued.

"I do not foresee any trouble for this trip, but if there should be, I want you, and so my name, well protected. I am sending Zafar along to be your personal bodyguard as he is mine."

Javed was surprised. "My Lord, I do not think this is necessary."

"And I say it is. Zafar, you are to go on this trip and from beginning to end you're to protect Javed as if he were me. I dare say, there will be little trouble and Javed should be easy to protect."

"As you wish, Master," said Zafar in his deep booming voice.

"You may go now, Zafar," said Omid. Zafar gave a deep bow to his master and then left the room.

"Now Javed," said Omid. "Sit and tell me all the details of how things are coming along."

Javed obeyed and told Omid all about the day's progress. He was then obliged to eat with Omid. Before he was sent away for the night Omid told him, "Tomorrow morning Arman, Kian, Mohsem, Hashem, Utabar, and Malek will come here to discuss further plans and tell what gifts they plan to take. I want you present for that meeting."

"Yes, my Lord," answered Javed before he left for his own mat to, hopefully, get some better sleep than the night before. He was very tired this night because of his lack of sleep. His mind was still exceedingly full though.

At mid-day the other six Magi showed up. Javed stood behind Omid as they were ushered in. The first thing to be discussed was the route of the journey. Omid did not need to know how they were going, but they still wished to tell him. Soon maps were laid out and roads talked of. It was decided that they would follow the great rivers and stay within the Parthian Empire as long as possible. Then they would continue down toward Jerusalem but stay out of the Roman Empire as long as possible.

Their destination for now was Jerusalem. This was the leading holy city of the Jews and the most likely of places to find the child. Since the child was believed to be royalty, they would go to the current king, Herod. If for some reason this child was not of Herod's family, and not in Jerusalem, surely the Jews there would know where this child was born. Omid gave them a word of advice.

"This child is not of Herod's family, for Herod is not a Jew and this child more will be."

Then came the discussion of what gifts were to be taken. Arman, Mohsem, and Hashem decided to go together and give a combined wealth of gold. Gold was an acceptable gift for any king as well as a customary one. Kian, Utabar, and Malek, too, were to combine in giving one gift. They would give frankincense. Frankincense was commonly used in sacrifices, including among the Jews. Utabar, who studied medicine specifically, also claimed it had healing qualities. This would be an acceptable gift as well, and Omid approved of them both.

Hashem then turned to Omid and asked, "And what gift do you wish to send along with us my Lord, Omid?"

"Javed will be in charge of my gift and of the personal giving of it to the child in my name," said Omid. "I will be sending myrrh." All eyes looked to Omid in surprise.

"Myrrh, Omid?" asked Arman. "True it is a gift that can be gotten in our country readily, as are our gifts. But my Lord, the Jews use myrrh in the burial of the dead. It can be used as perfume, true, but I do not see them using it much like that."

"I know all of this, Arman, but I still intend to send it. I have my reasons," stated Omid, and that was the end of it. Though all the others were puzzled by this, no one questioned further, at least not to Omid. If Omid wished to send myrrh, then they would take myrrh in his name.

A few more things were discussed before the meeting broke up. It was determined that they would have all they needed, and all would be ready in a week's time. Then, if the skies foretold no evil, they would leave. They would travel by day, for there would be no reason to travel by night, not to mention it would be more dangerous. Soon Javed's great journey would begin.

The next week was hectic crazy. Javed was busy or busier than anyone else. He had to help with all the many things that had to be done as well as see to extra things for himself since he was going. He found out he was to ride a large bay steed. He would also have another horse that would carry everything he would need as well as the Hebrew scrolls that Omid was to send with him. It would also carry Omid's precious gift of myrrh.

Javed was not taking much with him, especially compared with some of the other Magi. They all had several horses to carry their personal things. There were also horses carrying tents and all they would need to live on, on the road. There were also spare horses for riding and for packing to switch if needed or if something should happen.

Finally the day they were to leave arrived. The skies had predicted nothing on the nights before, so they were to be sent out. Javed was dressed in his normal slave garb, but he had better clothes packed for later in the trip.

Omid came out to send them off. One of the other young slave boys led him. This slave would take over most of Javed's duties while he was gone, Javed knew.

Before they left Omid had all the Magi who were going kneel before him, and he blessed them each individually. When he came to the end he stopped and called out, "Where is Javed?"

"Here my Lord," Javed answered as he came forward from where he had been standing with the other slaves who were in the back. He came forward and gave Omid a bow.

"Kneel, Javed," Omid commanded. Javed knelt, feeling as surprised as he was sure everyone else was. Omid laid his hands on Javed's head and began to speak. "Javed, I give you my blessing. You who have been like a son and grandson to me, I now send you out in my name. You are to go in my name to the greatest person who has been born in our time. May this trip bless you more than I ever can. May you come to a full understanding of the truth. May God reveal to you all you need to know. May you be blessed and may you bless others."

This blessing had been different from the others, and in a way Javed knew that Omid had been talking to him for just himself. Omid had not blessed him by the gods but by God. Omid had meant the one God of the Jews. He wanted Javed to come to a full understanding of this God.

Javed rose to his feet and bowed again to Omid. "Thank you, my Master. May all I do please you and bring honor to your name," Javed said.

"Thank you, Javed," Omid said. Then in a quieter voice, meant for Javed alone, he added, "May you learn to please God over all others, my child." Javed wished he could hug Omid, but this would not be proper. He was still a slave, so he settled for another bow even though Omid could not see it. Javed hoped he could hear it and somehow understand how much he meant to him. Soon the time came for all to mount their steeds and set out. Goodbyes and words of wisdom and advice where shouted back and forth as they left. Javed watched behind him until he could no longer see Omid, and then he turned his eyes forward. The journey had begun.

As the journey continued Javed got in the swing of travel. The first few days he was very sore, but as more days slipped by, his muscles hardened. One day, sometime later, Javed looked up from the scroll he held in his hand and surveyed the landscape around him. The day before they had left the valley of the Great River Ufrātu. They had followed it north as far as they needed to. Now they were to head south and east. They were trying to stay out of the desert as much as possible and in the fertile lands. The horses could stand some desert but these horses were not use to it, and it was easier on them all to stay out of the desert.

Javed glanced over his right shoulder. Behind him and a little to the side rode Zafar. He always stayed close to Javed. At night he did take his turn with the night watch. He would also participate in the training rehearsals they would have. Rahim, the leader of the bodyguards, deemed practice training some nights necessary to keep all the bodyguards sharp and alert.

At night when they would make camp, Javed had to help like all the other slaves. When his duties were done, he would sit down to eat and usually Zafar would eat with him. At first they did not really talk, but the longer the trip went the more they got use to each other and talked a little more.

Javed looked down at the scroll in his hand. He had found that the long day's ride was indeed long and there was not much to do. In the evening, it was late when they stopped and he had other things to do as well as being tired. Omid wanted him to study the Jewish Scriptures he had sent along, and Javed had found that during the day as he rode was the best time. He would select one scroll in the morning and would read it as he rode. He would read it over and over until he knew it all and had a fairly good understanding of it. A few of the scrolls he would take two days in a row until he was sure he had them down. Some of the smaller scrolls he would nearly have memorized by the end of the day.

Javed just wished he had someone he could discuss them with. Zafar was not the type to discuss religion of any kind. Zafar just did not talk much. Malek was the scholarly one of the Magi, but he studied all sorts of things from many peoples. He did not believe any of them. Javed wanted to better understand to see if this was what he did want to believe. Most of it he understood but there was nothing like talking it over with someone who understands where you are coming from and where you want to go. The big question on his mind was whether the Jewish God would accept him? He knew there were other peoples who had been taught that by the Jewish people but would their God accept one such as him, with his background in the study of stars and all?

They stayed out of the Roman Empire as long as they could, but eventually they had to enter Roman territory and from there into the Jewish region of Judea. When they entered Roman territory they were questioned. The Magi assured the solders that they came peacefully and showed them the letter that their own King had sent with them saying they were there on an inquiry and came completely in peace. They were permitted to enter the land, but the soldiers looked suspiciously at all the bodyguards who had come along. There were nearly as many bodyguards as there were other people and even some of the slaves knew how to handle a sword.

Their travels brought them closer and closer to Jerusalem. The closer they got the more excited Javed became. He still looked forward most, though, to the journey's end. His freedom awaited him, but he

At the End of the Journey

still was excited to see the Holy City of the Jews and the prophetic child king.

Then one night when they made camp, all were informed that tomorrow they would arrive at Jerusalem. They were to dress in their very finest tomorrow and make all things and steeds as fine as possible. Extra time was spent that night by all the slaves to make everything ready. When Javed lay down to sleep, he wondered if he would be able to sleep for anticipation of the day to come. But long days made one tired and the extra work only added to it, and before long he was sound asleep. In the morning he was awakened earlier than normal and more things were done to make all ready.

First he brushed his mount over and over until he was spotlessly clean. Next he put on the finest outfit he had. His long fine robe resembled that of the true Magi in a small way and was much different from his normal plain traveling clothes. Before, he looked like every other slave, but today he looked more like a Magi in training. Even the other slaves were dressed better than normal. Lastly everything had to be neatly packed.

Finally they set out. The six Magi led the way with Javed right behind them, and sometimes riding in with them. Behind them came the other slaves with all their belongings and things on the pack horses. All around them were the bodyguards. They were truly a caravan to behold. At about mid-day they entered Jerusalem. Although the city was used to caravans coming from other lands, many people still stared at them. It would seem that they were not used to seeing people in such dress or on such mounts. It was not known that they were coming and so to have such a group just appear, caught the city by surprise. They were not far into the city when they were approached by a well-dressed man.

"How may your humble servant help you, my great and noble Lords? I am Simon, and I have a thorough knowledge of all areas of our most beloved city."

"We wish to speak with Herod, your current king. We understand he is here in your city at his palace," stated Kian before the man could say any more.

"Oh yes. Our most illustrious King Herod is gracing our city with his presence. Would you like me to show you the way to his grand palace?"

"That would be fine," said Arman.

"Then just follow me, Your Exaltedness," replied Simon. Javed bit down hard on his lip to keep from busting up laughing. He was not sure that that was even a word.

Simon guided them down the streets, but his mouth moved about twice as fast as his legs. He had no end of things to say, all from what street they were now on and where in the city they were, to what business or buildings they were passing and any gossip surrounding them to the wealth and the general health of the people.

Javed watched the Magi in front of him to see how they were taking their flamboyant guide. Utabar and Mohsem were having a hard time keeping from laughing and even Malek and Hashem were grinning. Kian would glance back at them with an agitated look on his face. Arman would give them a stern look whenever Utabar or Mohsem would snicker too loud, but Javed was sure he had seen a grin on his face a time or two.

Simon was true to his word, and he led them right before the gates to Herod's palace. Kian then tossed Simon a fine gold piece and said, "I thank you good man for your service. You may now go about your business."

Simon's face fell, obviously not wishing to be sent away now. "Your Majesties, I could act as your herald before our great King Herod, or..."

But Kian cut him off by raising his hand. "We thank you for your time and service to us, but we shall proceed alone from here to His Majesty King Herod of the Jews." And adding more quietly, "King for now anyway."

Simon looked sad and a bit confused for he heard Kian adding the "for now." Javed understood this because they were there to find the new King of the Jews.

Sulking, Simon walked away and the rest of them were ushered into the courtyard. Once they were inside the gates, guards came forward.

"What have you come for, and how may we help you, my Lords?" the chief guard asked.

"We seek an audience with your king and master, Herod," answered Arman.

"Follow me," the guard commanded. Slaves hurried forward to hold the horses as they dismounted. Javed got down as well and Kian waved him along. The personal slaves of all the Magi came as well as half of the bodyguards. They were ushered inside to one of the first large rooms. There the chief guard left them.

"I will go see if His Majesty the King will see you now," he said.

Javed gazed around him. The palace was very fine, but he had seen just as fine and better already in his days. He had been to the Parthian king's palace. This one was different though. The style, he knew, was of a different kind, and he expected it was more Roman as well. He did his best not to stare, though, and behave more as the other Magi did.

They waited for a time before the chief guard reappeared.

"If you will come this way, please, My Lords," he said and led them down more hallways until they at last came to a large room filled with many people. On the far end of the room was an older man well propped up by cushions. The guard led them straight up to this man. When they were presented to the king they all gave him a low bow.

King Herod looked them over, and then spoke, "You are wiseman from Parthian, are you not?" They answered in the affirmative. "Well how can I and my kingdom help you?" he said.

Then they explained that they had come seeking the child who had been born to be the King of the Jews. They knew he had been born because they had seen his star rise in the East. They had come to pay homage to this new king.

When they had finished speaking the room was dead still and as quiet as a tomb. Every eye was turned on them and shock and surprise were on most faces. Kian was the first to break the silence. "I take this to mean the child is not here."

One of the King's advisers who was standing close to him responded, "Most certainly not. We have no knowledge of such a child having been born."

It was the Magi's turn to be surprised. They knew there was a possibility that the child may not be at this palace, but they thought that for sure these people would know where the child was. Javed's mind was sent into a whirl. What now? What did they do? How would this affect him?

Herod, who seemed to have been deep in thought, roused himself and spoke. "You are sure that this child has been born?"

"Most certainly," answered Arman.

"Well that settles it," said the King in suddenly a seemingly better attitude. "You will all stay here as my guests until this child is found. I shall do all in my power to find him. And in the meantime I hope you all will grace us with your presence here at my palace."

The Magi looked at each other then Arman answered, "It is a most gracious offer Your Majesty, and we accept. Your help in finding this precious child will be most helpful."

"Excellent!" shouted Herod. He then commanded that they should be shown to such and such rooms and given whatever they wished. Their horses were also to be given the best of care.

Several slaves stepped forward and led them back out of the throne room. Once they left the room, Kian stopped them and requested they be taken back outside so they could fetch their own people and get their things as well. The servants bowed in agreement and led them back outside. The Magi then explained to those who had remained outside what was going on. They then gathered their things and returned back inside. The horses were turned over to the waiting groomsmen.

Inside the palace, they were led down halls and corridors for a long way. Javed realized they were being led to one of the far wings of the palace, and he doubted he could find his way back out. When they reached their destination they were shown into two very fine and lavish rooms that were connected. It was soon determined that the larger and finer of the two rooms would be the six Magi's room and the lesser would be for the slaves and bodyguards. The bodyguards were then stationed on the inside and outside of all the doors and by the windows as well. Things were unpacked and set up to the liking of the Magi.

Javed managed to slip in a nap after all the work was done, for he found he was rather tired.

In the evening the six Magi were invited to dine with the King. Their bodyguards went with them. Javed remained with the rest of the slaves. He was not a free man yet and so it would not be right for him to go along. However, when the Magi returned they said they wished they had taken Javed with them to represent Omid.

As night fell, all went to their places and rooms to sleep. Javed found, however, that he could not sleep. He had gotten a nap during the day and he had lots on his mind now. They had reached Jerusalem, the Holy City. Javed had looked at this as being their destination although he had known, as the others did, that the child might not be here. However the Jews seemed to know nothing about this child having been born. Could they find him? And what happened if they could not? Would they be forced to go home in disgrace? And what would that mean for him? Would he still get his freedom? Would he have to tell Omid, "Master, I have failed you. I do not deserve to be set free." That thought made his heart sink like a stone. If they did not find this child there was no way he could earn his freedom. Or was there?

Javed opened his eyes wide and stared at the ceiling. What could he do that would earn him his freedom from this trip if they did not find the child? Well, he could give a very detailed account of all their travels and of Jerusalem and of this palace. But, Javed realized that would be expected anyway. Then another idea came to him. What if he learned something new from the Scriptures? He had been studying them the whole trip, but he doubted he knew more than Omid.

"It would need to be a lot more or something significant," Javed thought. He doubted he could find anything that would be worthy of obtaining his freedom but, hey, it was worth a try. Javed was wide awake and the scrolls lay near him, so he might as well try. Javed sat up and silently crawled off his bed mat. He selected several scrolls at random. Javed then stopped; it was not light enough to study in the room, and he would only disturb the others. Javed tried to think of what to do, when he noticed light from under the door. There would be torches in the hallway of course. He could sit down under one of them, and out in the hall he would not be disturbing anyone.

With the scrolls tucked under his arm he moved toward the door that led out into the hall. A bodyguard by the name of Niv was guarding the door. He gave Javed a stern look when he came to the door, so Javed decided he should explain.

"I cannot sleep so I will study in the hall where I will not disturb the others. Omid wanted me to study these things," Javed said. He brought up Omid for good measure. Niv nodded solemnly then and opened the door. Zafar was guarding the other side so Javed explained to him as well what he was doing. He then sat himself under a torch on the opposite wall and just a little down from the door so any noise he might make would not filter right under the door. He placed the scrolls on the ground and selected one. It was Isaiah. He had not read much of this one on the trip because Omid and he had studied it before he left. Starting at the beginning Javed began to read.

He had read for a time when he heard a noise. He stopped reading so he could listen. He then realized it was the sound of footsteps and they were coming toward him. Just beyond, from the opposite direction they had come, the hall curved. It was from there that the steps came. Javed sat and waited for the owner of the footsteps to appear. Then from around the corner came a young man. Javed guessed he might be only a little older then himself. The boy stopped abruptly, surprised at seeing him.

"Oh, I did not realize anyone would be out here," he said. He then stepped forward and gave Javed a bow.

Javed could not help but smile and say, "You need not bow to me, I am only a slave."

"Oh," said the other. He seemed to think a moment then added, "My name is Jacob."

"I am Javed," Javed answered.

"May I ask what you are doing?"

"I could not sleep so I decided I would come out here and study."

"What are you studying?"

"Actually I am studying some of your people's Holy Scriptures."

Jacob plopped himself down on the floor beside Javed. "You must have the Greek translation of them," he said.

"No," Javed answered and raised the scroll so Jacob could see. Jacob looked at it in surprise.

"You can read Hebrew?"

"Yes, I can read and speak many languages."

"Your master has taught you much then."

"I should explain more," said Javed. "My master is Omid, the greatest Magi there is alive. All the Magi here would agree. I am his personal slave, and I have come on this trip to represent him. My master Omid is blind so I read to him anything he wishes read, so I must know many languages."

"I see, but why are you reading them now?"

"My master Omid had me bring them along and wished for me to study them so I will know them well."

"But why are you reading them now, at this time of night?"

"I could not sleep so I decided to come out here to read so I would not disturb the others."

Jacob looked straight at him as if not satisfied with the answer. He then shook his head. "You must really enjoy studying to just read about a religion that is not your own."

Javed thought for a split second of whether to tell this boy more or not. He decided it could not hurt. "You know why we are here, don't you?" Javed asked.

"Yes, you all believe that the Messiah has been born and wish to pay homage to him."

"Yes, but no one here seems to know anything about it. What if we cannot find this child? You see, I have been promised my freedom on the return from this trip. But if we cannot find this child, what will I have to offer to my Master? I will not receive my freedom. I was thinking, though, that he wanted me to study these Scriptures. If I could find something in the Scriptures that my Master did not know about or something like that maybe I could still get my freedom. But that is all very unlikely for my Master knows nearly all there is to know, I think."

Jacob was silent and thought for a moment. He then turned to Javed and said, "Are you sure that this Messianic baby has been born?"

"Oh, yes, there is no question about that," Javed answered.

"Well, then Herod will search until it is found. Or he will die trying," Jacob said almost sadly.

Javed felt relieved. Jacob seemed very sure that King Herod would find the child. His freedom seemed secure once more.

"You could stop studying the scriptures tonight I think," said Jacob interrupting Javed's thoughts. Jacob stopped then and looked at Javed. "Why did your master want you to study our Scriptures?" he asked. "I suppose so you could better understand our people, and what you would be going into," added Jacob.

"No, not really," answered Javed. "You see, my master Omid believes as your people do, I think. He follows your Scriptures and does what it says as much as he can. He hopes that I will as well. He wants me to read so I may better understand everything that your people believe."

Jacob's eyebrows shot up in surprise at this. "Really," he said.

"Yes, but," Javed stopped and looked at Jacob. "I have questions and many things I wish to talk over with someone. Could…Could I talk to you?"

"Of course," said Jacob happily.

"You don't have anything you have to do? I mean you were just walking along and then stopped."

Jacob smiled. "I could not sleep like you so I decided to walk by here. I knew you were here and I wanted to see what I could see, even if it was just your guards," he said with a glance toward Zafar.

Javed smiled. Zafar seemed to not even know they existed but Javed knew that nothing they said had escaped him.

"Well, I know your God made everything and everyone in essence," started Javed. "But starting with Abraham, God separated the people. He made your people a set apart people. From Abraham, to Isaac, and from Isaac to his son Jacob, and from Jacob his twelve sons, and from them came the people of the Jews. The Jews are His holy and chosen people, chosen, set apart, and special, for Him. You have your own laws and customs that God has given you. My question is can an outsider really become like you? I mean can an outsider really become, well, Jewish? I know there are those who have. But is it truly possible?"

Jacob was thoughtful for a minute. "I believe one can," he finally said.

"But how can you be sure?" questioned Javed.

"Well, have you ever heard the story of Ruth?"

"Yes."

"Well, Ruth was an outsider, but she gave up everything to stay with her mother-in-law Naomi. She said that Naomi's home would be her home; Naomi's people would be her people; and Naomi's God, her God. She gave up all she had known to follow Naomi. She was accepted into the Jewish community, especially when she married Boaz."

"But what about someone like me? I know some of the studies that the Magi do, and I know there are some that would not be approved of by the Jewish law. I could leave all of that behind but I would already be tainted, so to speak. Could God ever forgive or overlook that?"

"There is also Rahab. Do you know about her?"

"I think I remember that name. Who or what exactly did she do again?"

"She lived in the city of Jericho when the Israelites came into the Promised Land to claim it. She hid the Israelite spies, and she knew that they were there to spy out the city for its downfall. She already was sure that God was real and that He would let His people take the city. She asked that she and her family be saved for helping them. But the big thing was that she was a prostitute. She was a bad person in the eyes of the law. She was an outsider and a terrible sinner, but she was brought into the camp of the Israelites and became one. Also both Rahab and Ruth were in the line of David. If you want to look at it further, the Messiah is to come from the house and line of David. So this child you are looking for would have both of these women in his lineage.

"There was also Melchizedek. Do you know of him?"

Javed nodded. "He was during the time of Abraham and gave him gifts after a fight. He was a king or a priest."

"Yes, he was both. He also gave Abraham a blessing. He was a very great man, but he was a king of somewhere else. A place called Salem."

Javed was silent. He was not sure what to say. He had to think over all that Jacob had said. Jacob was silent again and seemed to be thinking. When Jacob did start talking, he just started reciting a Scripture. It said how the people of the nations gather as the people of God and of Abraham because all things on earth belong to God. And for this God is greatly exalted. He then told Javed this was in Psalms (Psalms 47:7-9).

"There are a lot of things in the Psalms that imply many peoples will come to God."

Both were silent again. Then Javed spoke, "I will have to think on all of this."

"You do that. But now I think I should go," said Jacob.

"Yea, me too," agreed Javed.

"Maybe we will meet again."

"I hope so, but if not goodbye, and thank you so much."

"You are welcome, and best of luck to you in everything."

Jacob left then, and Javed slipped back into his room and back to bed. He thought he would think on all that was said for a while, but he found he was rather tired and was soon asleep. Javed was allowed to sleep in that morning, and he rested some throughout the day. There was talk of him and some others watching the stars this coming night.

Throughout the day when Javed could let his mind wander, he would think back over everything that Jacob had said. Javed still wondered, though, if he could be truly accepted. All of these people had lived long ago. He had studied their Scriptures, but he knew there was still much he did not understand. And maybe the Jewish people would accept him but would their God? He seemed to have accepted the people they talked about but that was then. Could he, Javed, truly be accepted? He was truly an outsider from farther way than the others they had talked about. He was not a woman marrying into a great family. He was not an important person either. He was still a slave now. The child they were looking for was the Messiah. He would be a child, but his family would not be. Would they accept him? He was there to represent Omid. Would they only see Omid's gift or would they take notice of him? Most likely not, he was a slave after all. Oh, could he ever be truly accepted? His head seemed to spin without getting to any real conclusions.

Most of the day was spent without anything being accomplished on their side. They heard nothing and were told nothing. In the late afternoon though, things started to move. Javed was sitting with the rest of the Magi writing down a few lines for Omid. At this point, admitted into their presence, was a guard.

"His Majesty King Herod requests a private meeting with you, my Lords. If you will come with me, I will take you to him. He also requested that you bring your charts and all information you may have on this mysterious star you spoke of."

"We humbly accept; let us gather our things," answered Armand. He then turned to Javed and said, "You will come with us this time."

"Yes, my Lord" Javed answered as a shock of excitement went through him. He was not sure if he would be allowed to come and now he had been told he would.

The guard, however, looked at him in a disdainful manner. "His Majesty asked that only those who are Magi come,"

"Javed is the representative of Omid, a far greater Magi then ourselves. We very much wish for him to accompany us. We will also be bringing our own guards," stated Arman very matter-of-factly.

The guard bowed in respect and submission to their wishes. In a few minutes the things they needed were gotten, and they followed the guard out of the room. They were not led back the way they had first come. Rather they were taken down various hallways and up stairs and all around.

Finally they were brought to a stop before a doorway, and the guard requested admission before letting them all enter. When they entered, Javed realized this must be one of King Herod's personal chambers. The King himself lay before them on a couch, of sorts, surrounded and propped up with many pillows. Other then Herod, only two slaves were in the room. Herod waved a hand to welcome them, and they all gave him a low bow.

"Welcome my friends, and many thanks for coming as I asked," said King Herod.

"How can we help you, O King?" said Kian.

"You spoke of a star the first time we met. I have a great curiosity about it. Would you so greatly honor me and help me to know all that you know of this star?" Then the charts were brought out. They showed where the star had first appeared and what sort of things it had done. Herod listened with great interest to all they told him.

"And when exactly did this star first appear? What day and how long ago was it," King Herod asked. The exact time was given. Herod then raised an arm and proclaimed, "My friends, you have been most helpful, and so it is my turn to tell you all I know, for I have not been idle this day. As soon as I was told by you of your plight, I arranged, this day, a meeting with all of our priests and scribes and anyone who might have knowledge of where the Messiah, who all of Judea is anxious for, is to be born. After much talk and examining of the Holy Scriptures it was made known, through the prophet Micah, that the Messiah is to be born in Bethlehem."

Everyone was surprised at this. They had not known this information could be gotten so soon. To have their destination proclaimed was a cause for great joy.

"Oh, King Herod, we thank you with all our hearts. It only remains to be asked where this great city of Bethlehem is. I have heard the name, but I do not know where it lies," said the ever-thinking Malek.

"I will gladly tell you where the town of Bethlehem lies, but first I must ask one favor of you."

"It would be an honor to do something for you, O King. Ask away" said Kian.

"As you can well see, I am not in good health. I travel as little as possible now. However your information of this baby Messiah has filled me with great joy," said King Herod. He continued on in a lengthy speech which amounted to him besieging them to come back and tell him exactly where the child was so he could go and see the child too. This was readily agreed to. Once this was agreed upon, King Herod gave them directions to Bethlehem. They were to pass through the Gennath Gate which was nearest to them then go west out of the city. The road that led from there would turn and head south and would go directly to Bethlehem. It was only a mere six-ish miles away.

"We thank you again, O King. Now if we can be escorted back to our rooms, we will pack our things and be on our way," stated Arman.

"Yet today?!" Surely you will wait until tomorrow? It will be dark before long," said King Herod in astonishment.

"Why wait, O King? We have not that much to pack and are accustomed to doing it all quickly," answered Kian.

"As you wish then, but you are welcome to stay as long as you'd like," said King Herod.

They were then escorted back to their rooms. The Magi announced that the town where the child was to be found was known, and they were leaving immediately. Everyone then was sent into a flurry of action. Herod sent other slaves and servants to assist them where they could. Right away some slaves were sent outside to get the steeds ready. Their things were wrapped up and packed in record time, but it was true, too, that they did not have to take down any tents. Soon they were all hurrying outside. Javed got only a quick glance of Jacob in which they could hardly give each other a smile and wave before they were gone from each other's sight.

Soon Javed was sitting back in the saddle of his horse, and they were all moving out of the palace courtyard and into the streets. They found the gate they needed and passed through. The road did turn south and went right by Herod's palace. Soon they were beyond the city and darkness was falling fast.

Javed looked up at the night sky that was filling with stars and felt excitement rising in him. Suddenly he saw something that made his eyes grow big. He looked at it carefully to make sure, then he urged his mount forward at almost a run to get up with the Magi.

"My Lords," he shouted with excitement as he slowed his steed in their midst. "Look," he said pointing up to the sky. There, gleaming down on them, was the special star. It had moved from where it had been seen last to a new place, nearly over top of them. Every eye turned up to the sky and the whole caravan was brought to a stop.

"May the gods be praised," shouted Kian and a chorus of agreement followed. Javed almost said it as well but stopped. After thinking he added in a quiet voice to himself, "Thank you, God of Abraham, Isaac, and Jacob. If this is your doing and you are the only God there is, then you are the one who deserves the praise."

Everyone was talking and watching the star when Arman shouted out, "By all the god's and powers, it's moving!" The others soon agreed that they thought it was too! "Then let us follow it. It is going south toward this Bethlehem. Let us see if that is where it goes, then we will know for sure we are on the right path."

With all eyes still looking steadily up to the sky, and on one star, they slowly began to travel again. Everyone was full of excitement and even the horses could feel it and became antsy. They had also been shut up for too long. Before long a small town could be seen before them.

"This is Bethlehem," announced Malek.

"And behold, the star has stopped! It seems to be over one area," pointed Arman.

"Let us follow it there," said Hashem.

All were in ready agreement, and they hurried on toward the town and the area where the star had stopped. Soon they were winding through the streets of the town. Few people were out anymore but some peaked out from inside their houses. Javed's pulse was racing to see where the star was leading them. Finally, they stopped before a house by Arman. The star was directly overhead. It had not moved and seemed to shine down on this house above any other.

Javed then looked at the house. It was very plain and simple. No different than any of the other houses around it. In fact they all seemed rather poor. All the houses Javed had seen in Jerusalem had looked better, and they had passed finer ones in this town as they had ridden along. The thought did raise in his mind, "Could this great Messiah child really be here?"

He did not have time to think on this much though. They were all dismounting. Kian then turned to him and said, "You will come in with us."

"I will?" answered Javed rather surprised at the sudden thought.

"Of course, you represent Omid and must present his gift. You had better go get it."

Javed hurried and got Omid's gift which had been so carefully packed away. He now carefully drew the vessel forth. He gathered with the rest of the Magi who were standing before the door. Kian then stepped forward and knocked on the door. The door opened by a rather young looking man.

"Is there a young child here?" asked Kian.

"Yes," the man answered rather surprised.

"Is he the one born King of the Jews?"

The man still looked surprised but a knowing look seemed to be there too. "We believe him to be the promised Messiah," he answered.

"May we see him, for we have traveled far to pay him homage?"

With a wave of his hand in the man said, "Please come in. You are welcome."

He led them from the door into a room that appeared to be the main living area of the house. Against one wall stood a girl, or rather a young woman, with a little boy in her arms. The man addressed the woman. "Mary, they have come to see Jesus."

Mary stepped forward and the man went to stand behind her with his hands on her shoulders. "This is my wife, Mary," he said. "And this is Jesus, whom she is holding."

It was then that all the Magi bowed to the ground before the child. When they rose all the Magi began to give speeches which amounted to that they had seen his star and had come to seek him to pay him homage knowing how great he was. Then Arman, Mohsem, and Hashem had their gift of gold presented. It was obvious that the man and woman were surprised by this. Kian, Utabar, and Malek then had their gift of frankincense brought forward. Again the parents were surprised. Then the Magi looked at Javed, and he knew it was his turn.

He stepped forward nervously and said, "I come in the name of Omid, the leader of all the Magi in the Parthian Empire. He, unfortunately, could not come on this trip to see his Majesty, so he has sent me, his humble slave, Javed, to present his gift of myrrh." At this Javed set the vessel down with the other gifts. The parents looked surprised and confused at this but thanked them all whole-heartedly for the gifts.

Then Mary stepped forward with Jesus so all the Magi could see him better and touch him if they wished. Jesus did not seem to know what to make of all these strong faces as he stared at them from the safety of his mother's arms. When they came to Javed, Jesus seemed to look him up and down then to everyone's surprise he held out his small arms towards Javed.

"He wants you to hold him," said Mary smiling. Rather surprised, Javed held out his arms slightly and suddenly found Jesus being passed to him. Javed was surprised and was not sure what to do. He stared down into the little face, and Jesus stared right back. Then Jesus smiled and reached up his little hands to pat Javed's face. Javed could not help but chuckle. He looked up to see Mary and the young man, who, he thought he had heard, was named Joseph, smiling at him. The other Magi were looking on too. They seemed a little envious but were smiling.

"He likes you," reassured Mary. As if in confirmation, Jesus let out a shriek of pleasure and laughter as he flapped his arms. He then leaned his head down on Javed's chest and half seemed to hug him. Javed felt his heart swell. He was accepted by this child and even chosen above all the others. Too soon, Jesus raised his head and held back out his arms to his mother. Javed handed him back to Mary but wished he could hold him forever.

"Can we offer you something, food or drink?" asked Joseph.

"Oh, no," replied Kian. "It is late, but we could not wait to set our eyes on the one we have come so far to see. But now we will go. We will camp out in the open tonight."

Nothing the couple could say would persuade them otherwise. Javed was not sure if they would come back in the morning or not. Nothing was said. Mary, Joseph, and Jesus accompanied them outside where all could see Jesus. When they did see him they all bowed as well. Joseph picked him up and held him high over his head so they could see him better. Jesus kicked his legs and flapped his arms letting out another loud shriek to the delight of all. All too soon it seemed they were remounting their steeds and riding away. Javed took one quick look over his shoulder at them standing in the doorway of their home as they all rode away. He would never forget this night.

It was also true, too, that this night was not over yet either. They made camp in the fields outside Bethlehem. Camp was soon made and all settled down for the night. Javed was not sure if they would return to see Jesus in the morning or not. Javed certainly hoped they would. He lay down to sleep like everyone else, but his mind was not yet ready to sleep. There were too many things that needed to be thought over and figured out.

He thought about little Jesus and his family. They were obviously very poor. At least they had been. They were not as much after tonight. They were common people, about as far opposite as one could get from King Herod as anyone in Judea could be. Jesus, too, was almost helpless. He still had to rely on others for everything. And his parents, they were so young. Nothing of what he had seen tonight was what he expected. They were poor, common, and so young. Javed had known that the child would be little, but seeing Jesus put it into perspective. And yet they were so accepting. Jesus had chosen to come to them over all others. And his parents had not seemed to mind at all. Most looked at the others as the real Magi and so important, and he was just a slave. Jesus may not have been able to tell the differences yet but surely his parents could. He had even said he was a slave, but they had had no problem with Jesus going to him. It showed for sure that at least some Jewish people could accept outsiders.

But, what about God? Well this Jesus was the Messiah. The Messiah was to be a great leader and save the Jewish nation. He came from the line of David and was to inherit David's throne forever. He was promised by God and was without a doubt an instrument of God. God could have had him born into any family, but it was this one that God chose. They, with all their youth and poverty, had been chosen by God to be the parents of the Messiah. So, if God chose them, and they accepted Javed, God likely would accept him too.

Javed sat straight up from where he lay. It was not guaranteed to work that way, but it seemed so. Javed looked up; even though the tent blocked his view, he felt that was the best place to look.

"God," he whispered into the darkness. "My name is Javed and I am an outsider. I don't come from the right people, nation, or any of that. I don't know if you can hear me or if I can talk to You like this, but...I want to...to believe in You, and if possible, belong to You. I know I come from a land of other gods and have lived all my life studying things You may not like. I will do or leave whatever You want me to. I don't know much, but I will try to learn more. I met Your Jesus, and I know You will do great things through Him. Could You...could You take me and make me Yours too?"

Javed then felt strange, like he was suddenly peaceful. He felt for sure that God had heard him, and he was accepted. He was not sure what would happen next but it would be okay. Javed lay back down and soon felt tears falling out of the corners of his eyes. They were happy tears though, and he had never felt this way before. Before long he was sleeping peacefully.

It was still dark when Javed sat straight up again from where he had been laying. His body was wet with a cold sweat. Images seemed to still dance before his eyes for a second before they finally cleared, and he was sure he was awake. He then began to shake. He had never had such a dream before. Or had it been a vision? In a second he decided he needed to talk to someone about this. Kian would be the best choice and if not him, he would understand and know who Javed should talk to.

Javed wasted no time slipping out of his tent and going to Kian's. Before he reached it though, he saw someone else go in. When he got to Kian's tent, his bodyguard, Alam, stopped him.

"What do you want here?" he questioned.

"I must speak to Kian," answered Javed.

"Who is it, Alam?" called Kian from within.

"It is Omid's slave, Javed," answered Alam.

"Let him enter," was the call from within. Alam stepped aside and Javed went in. Javed was surprised when he looked around and saw that all the Magi were in the tent. Several of them looked very disturbed too. "Sit down, Javed," commanded Kian. Javed obeyed and Kian then asked, "Did you have a dream?"

"Yes."

"What was it?" Javed then told his whole dream which was still fresh in his mind.

"That is exactly what mine was too!" cried Mohsem.

"It is the same dream we all have had," said Hashem.

"But what does it mean?" asked Utabar. At once everyone began to talk and say what they thought the dream meant. Finally Kian raised his hand and called for silence. Slowly all calmed down to listen.

"I think one thing is obvious from this dream. We must not return to that King Herod and tell him where the precious child, Jesus, is. I do not think we should wait here any longer either. Our very presence could endanger his life. I think it's best if we leave as soon as possible. Let us draw out the maps and find a different route back to our own land. It will take some time before Herod realizes we are gone and not coming back to him. And I do not think he will make so bold a move as coming after us for that could cause a war. But the man is not known for his rashness as he is rather paranoid. We should leave the Roman Empire as soon as possible."

All agreed to this and soon plans were made. From there the rest of the camp was awakened and made aware that they were leaving now because of the dream. As the sun rose, they were quickly riding away from Bethlehem. Javed looked over his shoulder as the town disappeared from sight. He was sad they could not see Jesus again but was glad they had seen him and with their leaving, he should be safe. He smiled as he looked up. His life would never be the same.

Several weeks later:

The whole caravan was long out of the Roman Empire and well on their way home. Javed sat tall on his steed and looked forward to the journey's end. But in many ways, he knew this was also just the journey's beginning. He was on a new journey now, the journey of getting to know this new God that was his God. He knew he was accepted by this God even though he was an outsider and did not know much. He would strive to learn more and to do whatever he needed to for this God. He had made the decision that when they got home, he would stay with Omid until he died. Omid was the only family he had, and he knew there was a lot he could learn from Omid. When Omid passed, there would be nothing to hold him there anymore. Then he would go back to Jerusalem. He would watch for Jesus and follow him and do whatever he could for Jesus. He would learn all he could about God and do his best to follow whatever Jesus said to do. Javed smiled as he looked straight ahead and knew that one journey was coming to an end, but another was just beginning.

Forty-some years later:

Javed ushered his wife and children into the meeting room of the house. The room was nearly full already, but Javed know it would be fuller before they started. The followers of The Way often met in this house. The owner was an early follower and with such a large room in his house, he had soon opened it up for meetings.

Tonight would bring many followers and Javed guessed the room would be full to overflowing. None of the disciples were to be here tonight but there were to be two speakers that Javed very much wanted to hear. They said they both saw Jesus on the night he was born.

After an hour had passed, everyone that could be squeezed into the room had been squeezed in and then some. The service then started with singing and worship. Prayer request were made and praises were said. Finally, a man walked to the front of the room and began to speak.

"My name is Judea," he started. "I was present the night that Jesus was born. I want to start a little before that though. A years before this, my family died. Only my little sister, Hadassah (who is here tonight) and I were left. The village we lived in was hit by disease and was nearly wiped out. To this day I don't know what caused it, but at the time there was a lot of talk about why it came. It was even said to have been caused by God for one reason or another. After this my sister and I went to live with an older distant relative of ours in Bethlehem. He was a very good and Godly man, but he was not used to children, and in his house everyone worked. At that time, I was just bitter and angry. I gave up on God and thought there was no way that God cared for his people anymore. Maybe, just maybe, He could hear the prayers of the priestly and very good people, but I was sure that God cared nothing for the poor and common people. I did not think He even knew I existed. How could He have taken my family and those I loved if He knew I existed? I had tucked everything I felt inside and never let anyone see it. I had my sister, but I felt alone in many ways and I needed to be the strong one for her now. This would all change, thanks to a very young and poor man and woman and our baby Lord Jesus."

Judea then told about everything he had talked to Mary and Joseph about. In the end he said, "God kept His promise of sending the Messiah. He sent His angels to two poor and ordinary people. At least the world would have thought them ordinary. But it all showed me that God still cares, and not just for his people in general but for individuals too. He loves and cares about me. I can't tell you why my family died, but God still loves me and cares for me, this I am sure of. I still lived in Bethlehem when I heard of a man named Jesus doing great and powerful things. I knew it was the same Jesus, the Messiah. Some of the things He said were hard to take in. But I learned the truth and followed Him. I learned He was not just the Messiah but the Son of God. This made sense with all that I was told by Mary and Joseph.

"I leave you with this truth: no matter who you are, or what you have been through or thought about God, He still knows about you, and loves you. He loved you alone enough to die for you. You are loved and special to God."

There was a little talk after this, and then the next man stood up and began to speak.

"My name is Benjamin," he said. "Judea and I met briefly that night because I was with the shepherds. My story, too, begins before the night of Jesus' birth. I started out the very opposite of a shepherd. My family was of the priestly line, and we were very proud Sadducees. My father was in charge of the temple treasury. He was not the best father, but like most boys I looked up to him and wanted to be just like him. I was very proud, but I also tried very hard to get my father's approval which I felt I could never get. Then one day my world turned upside down. My father was caught stealing from the temple treasury and was stoned. It all happened very quickly, and I thank the Lord I was not there to see it.

Then my mother and I had to go live with my uncle and his family who had been very jealous of us. In a way they felt that they could get back at us and were now better than we were. My uncle decided I should become a shepherd and help with his sheep. This was a terrible blow to me at the time. I felt terrible about leaving my mother behind, and I thought my fate was unbearable. The old shepherd in charge of me, however, was very kind and helped me out a lot. He helped me to become a good shepherd, and he also helped me to understand God and the Scriptures better. I thought I was condemned for my father's sins. I thought I knew so much, but there was so much I did not know or had been taught wrong."

Benjamin talked about all he had learned and then about the night of Jesus' birth. He saw and was talked to by angels. The shepherd then had gone and found Jesus. "God showed me that I was still worthy, even if I was unworthy in the eyes of all others. I was a shepherd and had finally learned to accept it and was accepted by the whole group. But in the eyes of the rest of the world I was at the bottom of the pile. I was as far from being respectable and worthy as one could get. But God sent His angels to us.

"I was a shepherd for several years after that. I learned humility in that and the importance of hard work. My mother eventually remarried, and I was allowed to come home. My new father is a very good man, and both of them are sitting here tonight. I am not as high in society as I once was. Nor am I at the bottom, but I have learned to be content wherever I am and with whatever I have. I still talk to and try to help those shepherds I knew, as well as others. I have learned not to look down on others.

"I, too, will leave you with a truth. You might be unworthy but no one is seen as unworthy to God. It does not matter what you have done, or even not done. You can be the best of the best or the worst of the worst. God still loves you and wants you as His child. Don't be afraid to come to God. He is waiting for you with open arms. He will wipe away all your sins. That is what Jesus died on the cross for. God loves you."

There was much talk that followed and Javed soaked up every word. He knew he could have told his story too but did not think now was the time. The meeting slowly broke up and all started heading home. Javed walked with his family down the streets to their own home. He thought back over the years. When he had first come, he had still struggled with the idea of whether he could do enough to be truly accepted. He had been very zealous for God like many postulates. Then he had gone to hear Jesus one time and learned it was the same Jesus. He had started following Him and soaking up everything He said. He had been shocked and crushed when Jesus was killed and skeptical when he heard He lived again. When he truly knew it was true, he rejoiced.

He now understood he did not have to work or do more to get on God's side because he was an outcast. God accepted him the way he was. Outcasts were no longer outcasts with Jesus. Jesus loved him. He was not to sin and was to live for Him but works could never save a person. One could never do enough or be the right person for God. He accepts us the way we are. We in return live for Him. By grace we get what we do not deserve and go from outcast to Child of God.

Javed smiled. This life is one journey and at this journey's end, Jesus will be waiting to welcome us home, in His eternal love.

Cleo Lael

End Notes

Edited by James Orr, published in 1939 by Wm. B. Eerdmans Publishing Co.

Christie, W. M. "Inn in the International Standard Bible Encylopedia. "*International Standard Bible Encyclopedia Online*. International Standard Bible Encyclopedia Online, 1939. Web. 10 Apr. 2016. <http://www.internationalstandardblible.com/I/inn.html>.

"Manners & Customs: Shepherds Shepherds in the Ancient World." N.p., n.d. Web. 20 Feb. 2014. <http://www.bible-history.com/links.php?cat=39&sub=414&cat_name=Manners+%26+Customs&subcat_name=Shepherds>.

Ross, Allen. "3. The Sadducees." *Bible.org*. Bible.org, 12 Apr. 2006. Web. 21 Feb. 2014. <https://bible.org/seriespage/sadducees>.

Schoenberg, Shira. "Ancient Jewish History: The Sanhedrin." *The Sanhedrin*. American-Israeli Cooperative Enterprice, n.d. Web. 21 Feb. 2014. <http://www.jewishvirtuallibrary.org/jsource/Judaism/Sanhedrin.html>.

Tunsil, Bruce. "What Did the Sadducees Believe?" *Answers*. Instant Checkmate, n.d. Web. 22 Feb. 2014. <http://wiki.answers.com/Q/What_did_the_Sadducees_believe>.

Werner, Barnes. "Education." *Education In Jesus' Time*. Sites.google.com, 01 Dec. 2011. Web. 23 Feb. 2014. <https://sites.google.com/site/educationinjesustime/>.

Larson, Frederick A. "To Stop a Star." *The Star of Bethlehem*. Frederick A. Larson, 2016. Web. 10 Apr. 2016. <http://www.bethlehemstar.net/starry-dance/to-stop-a-star/>.

McGarvey, J. W. "Eastern Wise-Men, or Magi, Visit Jesus, the New-Born King." *Biblehub*. The Four-Fold Gospel — J. W. McGarvey, n.d.

Web. 20 Nov. 2014. <http://biblehub.com/library/mcgarvey/the_four-fold_gospel/xiii_eastern_wise-men_or_magi.htm>.

MacArthur, John F. Jr. *The Miracle of Christmas*. Zondervan Publishing House, Michigan: Grand Rapids, 1995.

"Parthian Empire." *Wikipedia*. Wikimedia Foundation, n.d. Web. 02 Dec. 2014. <https://en.wikipedia.org/wiki/Parthian_Empire>.

Kirby, Peter. "Historical Jesus Theories." *Early Christian Writings*. 2016. 10 Apr. 2016 <http://www.earlychristianwritings.com/text/1clement-hoole.html>.

Dingdong. "The+roman+empire+in+the+first+century - Google Search."*The+roman+empire+in+the+first+century - Google Search*. History Of Medieval Europe, n.d. Web. 10 Apr. 2016. <https://www.google.com/search?q=the%2Broman%2Bempire%2Bin%2Bthe%2Bfirst%2Bcentury&espv=2&source=lnms&tbm=isch&sa=X&ei=MbGtU-iSJMPZoASRnYD4Bg&ved=0CAcQ_AUoAg&biw=1366&bih=643#facrc=_&imgdii=_&imgrc=wSifwFfjMtc63M%253A%3BFfuclEzQDXnJxM%3Bhttp%253A%252F%252Fgbgm-umc.org%252Fumw%252Fcorinthians%252Fmaps%252Fempire.gif%3Bhttp%253A%252F%252Fgbgm-umc.org%252Fumw%252Fcorinthians%252Fempire.stm%3B600%3B406>.

For more information contact:

Cleo Lael
C/O Advantage Books
P.O. Box 160847
Altamonte Springs, FL 32716

info@advbooks.com

To purchase additional copies of this book visit our bookstore website at: www.advbookstore.com

Longwood, Florida, USA
"we bring dreams to life"™
www.advbookstore.com

www.ingramcontent.com/pod-product-compliance
Lightning Source LLC
Chambersburg PA
CBHW070532100426
42743CB00010B/2048